THE COMPETENT SWIMMER

A step-by-step teaching manual

Maureen Dyson
&
Judith Shapland

A & C Black · London

This book is dedicated to Steve Davies

Recently, ASA/STA recommendations for the safe teaching of diving have become more stringent than in the past.

The type of diving and practices described in this book should take place only in diving pits conforming to FINA (Federation Internationale Natation Amateur)/ASA standards.

In pools where the maximum vertical depth is 1.8m, beginner divers should be instructed only at this depth and solely in flat racing dives.

Teachers are urged to find out how these latest recommendations affect instruction in the pool they use and also to keep abreast of any further discussion relating to safety in the teaching of diving.

First published 1992 by
A & C Black (Publishers) Ltd
35 Bedford Row, London WC1R 4JH

A CIP catalogue record for this book
is available from the British Library.

Acknowledgements
Design by Tony De Saulles.
Illustrations by Tony de Saulles
and Simon Borrough.

Printed and bound in Great Britain by
Hollen Street Press Ltd of Slough.

Contents

The authors

Maureen Dyson trained as a Physical Education teacher at Lady Mabel College, Rotherham (Yorkshire), afterwards working with both primary and secondary school children in Cumberland, Yorkshire and Berkshire. Since 1973, she has been employed by Westmorland and Cumbria Education Authorities as a swimming teacher and is responsible for the swimming in the 27 primary schools in Kendal and district.

Judith Shapland trained at Lady Mabel College of Physical Education and has taught both secondary and primary school children in Wales, Australia and England. She is the Swimming Co-ordinator for Cumbria.

INTRODUCTION

This manual evolved in circumstances which must be familiar to many swimming teachers. Though continuing to provide swimming instruction for all children, the Cumbria Education Authority has been compelled by never-ending financial restraints to reduce and further reduce the number of pool visits, so that swimming is now taught for only two years at primary school. In addition, large classes have necessitated the enlistment of help from class teachers and/or parents who in the majority of cases have little or no swimming expertise.

Without intending it to be a substitute for STA or ASA teaching methods, the aim of the manual is to provide these co-operative and enthusiastic but unqualified helpers with simple schemes of work to guide their teaching and to ensure a continuing progress for the children in their groups.

Even if there were adequate time available to guide children through meaningful experimentation in and exploration of swimming activities, so as to bring about improvement to a variety of strokes and skills, it would be asking too much of helpers lacking a thorough knowledge of the subject to use such an approach.

Instead, and less dauntingly, the teaching can be delegated by providing information, expressed in lay terms, on how to build up a stroke or skill from its component parts whilst working with a group of children of the same stroke experience. Weekly instalments of lesson plans, with brief descriptions and simple illustrations, serve this purpose. These lesson plans have been thoroughly tested in Cumbria's teaching pools.

The programme of work, covering four strokes and a range of watermanship skills, has developed and been modified over a period of years. It has been used mainly in primary schools with mixed and single age classes from 2nd year juniors upwards, of between 30 and 40 pupils. The success rate in competent swimmers has been consistently around 99 per cent. For teaching purposes, the programme has been divided into shallow, middle and deep group sections, each section representing an ability group with specific strokes and skills to learn.

In the shallow group, the emphasis is on the gradual and thorough building up of breast stroke; a choice which rests on the conviction that this stroke, above all, is invaluable for survival in water. Experience shows that, whilst the initial learning of breast stroke can be difficult, once established, with its alternating 'work and rest' action and use of the stronger limbs for the main propulsion, it is less physically demanding than front or back crawl. A further advantage, for the nervous swimmer, is that the head can be held out of the water throughout the stroke. The shallow group section explains in detail how to build up this stroke using the 'Y, frog, I' teaching method.

The middle group section deals with the two back strokes and the deep-water skills of treading water; head-first surface-diving; shallow entry; underwater swimming; and the safe removal of clothing, as used in some survival situations.

Finally, the deep group section introduces front crawl and shallow dives, continues with stroke and survival skills improvement and the use of strengthening activities to increase stamina. Butterfly, being a purely competitive stroke, has not been included in the programme.

Confidence always increases as a by-product of stroke learning and from working in the company of class-mates. However, for the very timid or frightened child, water confidence activities are an essential preparation for enjoying and participating in the group work. There are numerous books on this subject and most teachers have their own favourite ploys for tempting the reluctant to wet their faces or float their feet. A short list of confidence-building activities precedes the introductory lesson.

In conclusion, it must be pointed out that the schemes might need modification to satisfy any ethnic considerations and that adaptations might have to be devised to suit individual pools. The manual would *not* be suitable for use in outdoor pools.

Reasons for teaching swimming

- Individuals who learn to swim can save their own or another person's life.

- Regular swimming promotes fitness and health and is recommended by doctors and physiotherapists as the best all-round exercise.

- Swimming places no stress or strain on the body as a result of the support of the water.

- Age is no restriction.

- Either individually or in a group, swimming can be recreational, competitive, or used in aqua-related activities.

Framework for assessment

To be judged competent, each child should be able to:

1 swim 25 metres with correct technique using each of the following strokes:
- breast stroke
- back crawl
- front crawl
- life-saving back stroke.

2 swim 800 metres using one or more strokes.

3 tread water for one minute.

4 mushroom-float for ten seconds.

5 straddle-entry into deep water.

6 surface dive and swim under water for 5 metres.

7 recover an object from 1 metre of water.

These skills serve as an introduction to life-saving and produce a range of stroke opportunities for exercise, competition and aqua-related activities. In addition they encourage efficiency of effort and elimination of stress and strain.

Framework for teaching and achievement

The most effective period for teaching swimming is the three-year period in primary schools from age 8 to 11: learning is rapid and easy; interest is high, and absenteeism is low. Teaching must be regular and of sufficient length to attain the objectives. A substantial success rate can be achieved within 30 hours by utilising 30 minutes each week for two consecutive school years (only six school days in a child's life).

The class teacher can use the body fitness and health aspects in cross-curricular links within the National Curriculum.

ORGANISATION

Beforehand

1 Issue pool regulations and needs for teachers/helpers, e.g. gymshoes, suitable clothes, whistle, class register.

2 Ask schools to do footchecks and hygiene before the first visit. Some may prefer the teacher to diagnose verrucae or athlete's foot.

3 Check and prepare equipment, e.g. armbands, floats.

4 Record the pool's dimensions – useful for measuring 100m circuits, 5m underwater swims, etc.

First day

1 Show teacher/helper:
- registration book
- emergency bell positions.

2 Tell children about:
- fire evacuation procedure
- pool safety rules
- areas of deep water in the pool.

3 Assess children by observing them whilst they have a go at simple activities in a safe depth, then sort them into groups for teaching. Three groups should be formed, if possible, i.e.:
Shallow:
- non-swimmers/weak swimmers (a few strokes)
- swimmers without a correct breast stroke.
Middle:
- swimmers with breast stroke (symmetrical; correct use of feet; an arm

action which stays ahead of swimmer) who are poor at treading water and have only one or no back stroke.
Deep:
• swimmers with breast stroke and two back strokes, who are good at treading water and confident to submerge to at least 1.8m.

Children in their first year of swimming may well be grouped as follows:
Shallow 1:
• very frightened, physically unco-ordinated, immature non-swimmers.
Shallow 2:
• slightly nervous but co-ordinated non-swimmers
• confident non-swimmers
• swimmers without breast stroke.
Middle:
• swimmers with breast stroke, as described above for middle and deep groups. Those who are already competent could, with the school's co-operation, come with an older group and do deep work, or could be extended by different means whilst working with the middle group.
   In this situation (two shallow and one middle group), using the most skilled teacher with the better shallow group, by the end of the second term you should be able to change to:
• new deep group
• middle
• shallow.
By the end of Term 5, there should be:
• deep group (original)
• deep group (new)
• middle.

SYLLABUS

Shallow group

Introduction to:
Breast stroke · Crawl kicking (front or back) · Submerging; breath control activities

Awards:
Beginner's badge · Swimming Teachers' Association (STA) distance awards – 5m, 10m, using breast stroke

Middle group

Improvement in:
Breast stroke

Introduction to:
Back crawl · Life-saving back stroke · Treading water · Mushroom-floating · Underwater swimming · Basic dive action *in* water · Head-first surface dive · Shallow entry from sitting on pool-edge · Swimming in clothes; undressing; float-making · Controlled deep water activities (end of Term 2)

Awards:
Improver's badge · Intermediate badge · Proficiency badge · STA distance awards 25m to 800m

Deep group

Strengthening:
All previously learnt strokes and watermanship activities

Introduction to:
Front crawl · Feet-first surface diving · Survival work · Diving from side

Awards:
Proficiency badge · Advanced Award (Year 6) · STA Survival Award — Bronze, Silver, Gold, Merit · STA Distance Awards — 800m to 5km

UNDERSTANDING THE LESSONS

Italic type — *comments or instructions intended for teacher's use.*

Roman type — instructions to be given to the children.

Illustrations — oval shapes on arms represent armbands.

√ do it this way
× not this way!

× 2 — suggested number of times to repeat the activity.

Supplementary activities — practices which recur throughout the lessons.
1 Life-saving back stroke (a dry-land practice).
2 Picking up a brick.
3 Safe removal of trousers.
4 Front crawl practices.
5 Safe removal of top over head.
6 Float-making.

Work sheets — appropriate lists of activities expressed in simple terms and displayed to occupy any group working on its own; for example:

● children lacking skill to accompany remainder of group into deep water, usually middle group
● relatively able groups — at times such groups, by working on their own, could free a teacher to concentrate on testing or to cover for the non-appearance of an expected teacher/helper.

Numbering the group — to avoid congestion caused by the whole group responding to instructions at the same time, the children are lined up along the pool-edge and are numbered in sequence, e.g. 1, 2, 3, 1, 2, 3, making sure that the children are aware of their number. At the beginning of each activity, the 1s set off first, followed at three-second intervals by the 2s and then the 3s.

Caterpillars – counting 'one caterpillar' gives a near estimation of the duration of one second.

T-mark – short line-marking across the end of the lane lines, which may not occur in all pools.

Shoulder/chin deep – the level of the water when the swimmers stand upright with their feet flat on the floor.

Abbreviations –
FC: front crawl
FFSD: feet-first surface dive
HFSD: head-first surface dive
LSBS: life-saving back stroke
MF: mushroom-float/ing
TW: tread water.

WATER CONFIDENCE ACTIVITIES

In armbands – keep it simple, make it fun! Suggest the children do the following.

1 Sit on pool-edge, feet dangling in water. Kick hard/gently alternately. Turn the pool into a Jacuzzi/a washing machine/the sea.

2 Try to splash the ceiling/the teacher!

3 Enter pool one at a time *(teacher very near – hold a hand if necessary),* counting the steps to the floor. *Place timid hands firmly on trough or rail. Make sure everything is all right before next child comes in.*

4 Pretend to be crabs – holding on to trough, slide feet sideways along floor, a step at a time. After four or five steps, go the other way. Can you be fast crabs this time?

5 Go skating/skiing. Hold trough with one hand and slide feet forwards one after the other. How about skating backwards?

6 You've dipped feet/knees/tummies; now dip arms/hands/ shoulders/neck/chin/nose/face/head and give them a wash!

7 *Walking on the pool-floor (walking on knees if it's a shallow pool):* paddle a canoe, first with one hand then with two.
Row it backwards, both hands at the same time.

8 Hold rail or rest hands on steps. How near the water can you put your chin? How high can you lift your feet? Can you hide your chin and show me your feet?

For the more confident (armbands on or off).
1 Bail out the boat – use a float to lift water over your head/shoulders.

2 *Skipping/running/hopping/jumping races – just a few metres.*

3 Dribbling a float with fingers/chin/nose/forehead, legs kicking at the surface to propel the swimmer forwards.

4 Can you stand on your float *(float on the floor)*? Jump off it and catch it before it reaches the surface.

5 Can you kneel/sit/handstand on your float?

6 With a partner – can you both duck under and smile at each other?
Did your partner smile or pull a face – or blow bubbles?

SHALLOW GROUP

There are 13 activities (see also pages 14–21) to be introduced gradually as indicated in the chart. Each week, start at the beginning and work through as far as possible making sure that the children have understood the aim of each activity.

First term

Week 1 – Introductory shallow lesson*

Activities	1	2	3	4	5	6	7	8	9	10	11	12	13
Week 2	✓	✓	✓	✓									
Week 3	✓	✓	✓	✓	✓	✓							
Week 4	✓	✓	✓	✓	✓	✓	✓						
Week 5		✓	✓		✓	✓	✓	✓	✓				
Week 6		✓	✓		✓	✓	✓	✓	✓	✓			
Week 7		✓	✓		✓		✓			✓	✓		
Week 8		✓	✓		✓		✓			✓		✓	✓
Week 9		✓	✓		✓					✓		✓	✓
Week 10		✓	✓		✓					✓		✓	✓

At this stage try swimming 5m breast stroke (badges are available).

---

* This type of lesson with simpler activities would be used for several weeks with a shallow group lacking in confidence.

Second term

The activities of greatest value are numbers 2, 3, 5, 10, 12, 13. Select the most suitable for the group, spending more time on 13 and aiming towards swimming 5m and 10m. Intersperse with plenty of water-confidence and submerging activities.

Third term

Children who have competently swum 10m of breast stroke begin middle group activities.

INTRODUCTORY SHALLOW LESSON

For children with confidence, but incorrect or no breast stroke.

Equipment

Two armbands on above elbows, two floats each.

1 Sit on pool edge, feet in water.

2 Slide in feet-first; face trough and hold it with both hands.

3 Float feet up behind. Kick legs up and down. Make a big splash.

Short rest.

Kick again, making a bigger splash.

4 *By numbers, repeat and see which group can make the biggest splash.*

5 With one float, go about 3 metres away from side. Face side. Kick legs up and down and **push** float with fingertips to side.

6 *Repeat, with the children pushing float with chin.*

7 With a float under each arm, lie on your back *(head back into water and look at ceiling, tummy up at surface).* Kick legs up and down gently, with toes pointed, knees **under** surface. Don't cycle. Pretend to kick a ball up into air.

8 On back, as before, try to return to side, by pushing against water with both feet at the same time.

9 *Armbands off, only if individual is confident.* **In a space, hide under the surface:**

one shoulder
both shoulders
chin
one ear
face
both ears
head.

10 Show above the surface:

one knee
one foot
both knees
seat
both feet.

11 Those who can:

go 3m from side, swim to side using favourite stroke and climb out.

SHALLOW GROUP ACTIVITIES

Introduce these practices from Week 2 onwards for those capable.

Equipment
Armbands on, above elbows.

1 *Sit group on pool-side, spaced out (**not** with feet dangling over pool-edge).*

Legs together, knees straight, slowly do the following.
(a) Frog.

All at the same time:

- bend knees outwards.
- slide feet apart, turning them out
- flex ankles.

(b) Push.

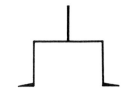

Big space *between heels.*

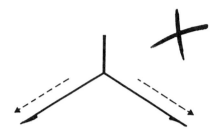 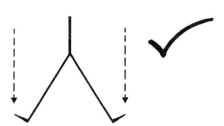

Keeping feet turned out and ankles flexed as long as possible, push feet forwards until knees are straight.

(c) Together.

×4 Keeping knees straight, slide legs together.

During this basic breast stroke leg action practice, check and correct individually.

2 With two floats each, sit on pool edge.
Number group in threes or fours and, by numbers, tell the children to slide in feet-first.

3 Take one float 5 metres from side (six big strides). Face side. Kicking legs up and down, push float to side with chin, nose or forehead.

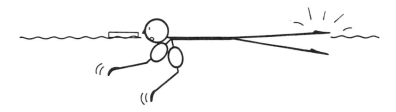

4 *In groups, by the same numbers.*
On back, one float under each arm, legs together, knees straight.
Tell the children to **frog and stop.**
Swimmers should frog their legs and hold frog position. Quickly check and correct if necessary and then **push forwards and slide together.**
Swimmers should keep their ankles flexed and feet turned out during push.
Repeat these two calls for half a width.
Return to side, still on back, kicking up and down; knees **under** surface, toes pointing.

5 On tummy, one float under each arm, holding floats well back to keep your feet near the surface.

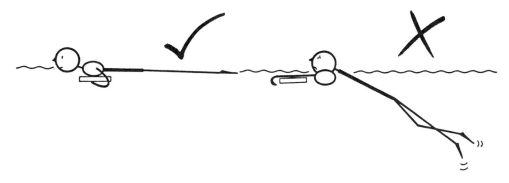

Then **frog and stop.** *Check positions individually.*
Push **back** and slide together, *for half a width and return.*
When frogging, lift feet up to surface, behind. **Do not** pull knees forwards under tummy.

During 'push back' keep feet **frogged** and knees **lifted outwards**.

Allowing a knee to drop down and turn in at beginning of push back creates an asymmetrical screw-kick: the leg screwing in will push down with the outer side of the foot leading, just after the other leg pushes back.

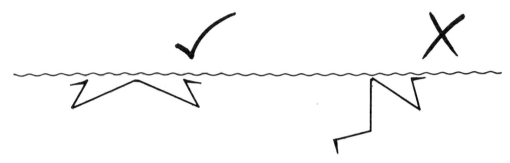

6 *Explain to the children that the next practice is the making of three shapes whilst floating on the tummy, and that by changing from one to another in the correct order, they will swim breast stroke. Space group out facing side.*

No floats. Try floating on tummy in:

(a) I-shape.
('I' for ice)

Palms facing floor.

(b) Y-shape.

Palms facing outwards.

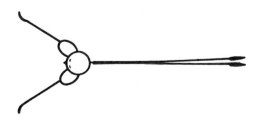

Feet tend to sink in I or Y-shape — this does not matter.

T-shapes or arrows are not correct.

Explain with group on pool-side, if need be, with a child on tummy.

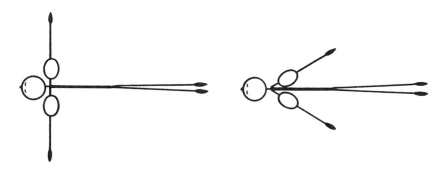

(c) 'Frog' shape.

Elbows tuck in to ribs. Hands together, palms down slightly ahead of chin, just under surface.

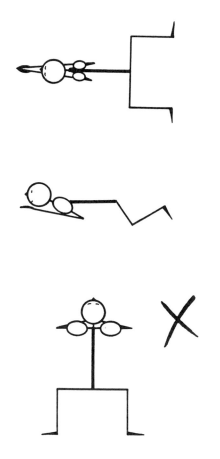

Try all three shapes – I and Y and frog – several times.

7 *By numbers from side, always set children off in I-shape.*
Now call out the three shapes **slowly**, *in this order:*

(2 half widths) Y, frog, I,   Y, frog, I *and so on.*

'Y' *is the initial* **small** *pull.*
'I' *is the glide* **finish** *to each stroke.*
Keep head up all the time.

8 *Explain how arms move from 'frog' to 'I', i.e.* by straightening forwards, thumbs together, palms down, which is one movement; *and how legs move from 'frog' to 'I', i.e.* by pushing back and sliding together – two movements which were practised before. *Though arms and legs set off into 'I' at same time, arms complete the change first.*

×6 Practise starting in frog shape and changing into I-shape.

(2 half widths) **9** *Without any prompting, let the group try Activity 7 again. In addition to any general confusion, most will miss out the I-shape! Discourage any head-down-in-water swimming. This could produce an incorrect use of arms and a flotation which destroys the need for a good leg action.*

(2 half widths) **10** *Call out shapes more quickly, giving I-shape a longer duration than Y and frog.*

11 *Stand group approx. 1m from and facing side with arms extended forwards, thumbs together, elbows straight, chin on surface.*
Step forwards and float to side in I-shape. Try to arrive with hands together and legs together and chin on surface. Blow out ×6 strongly through mouth whilst floating forwards.

12 Repeat Activity 11 with armbands off. *(Not the absolutely terrified and extremely unco-ordinated children – they will need more supported time in the water.)*

NB Children must be told **clearly** *to begin this step and glide with* **shoulders, arms and hands under surface,** *and to keep them* **under** *all the way to the side. They must also keep the* **head up** *Children should slide* **through** *water, not along top of it. Group must be reminded constantly.*

Children must be discouraged from jumping out of water to grab at trough. If they miss trough, after jumping out over surface, they will sink, not far – but alarmingly!

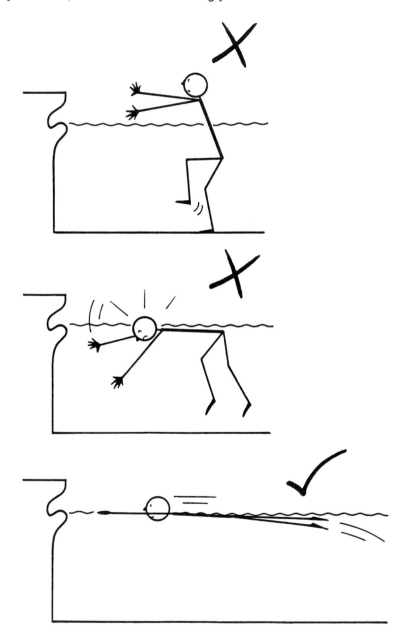

13 *Whilst nervous and unco-ordinated children continue to practise Activity 11 in armbands, the others should now move 2 metres back from side. Setting off with the step and glide just practised, which lifts feet off floor, they can try to complete one Y, Frog, I, with head up, before reaching side.*

When this has been achieved **correctly**, *move them back another metre, to try step and glide and two strokes and so on. Work the children independently now.*

Aim at correct stroke production rather than distance. At this stage, two correct strokes (with head up) are a bonus. One width of an incorrect stroke is a waste of effort. Head-down swimming must be prevented. It will cause an extended and therefore incorrect arm pull. Equally undesirable, with the head down the swimmer acquires a flotation which makes the proper use of feet and ankles unnecessary. Instead, encourage swimmers to blow out every time they make the I-shape, or every time their hands move forwards to begin another stroke, as a foundation for correct breathing and blowing, without exaggerated head noddings, later.

__Co-ordinated__ but nervous children, who are not able to pluck up courage and set off (this is the hurdle), can often be helped by the use of mini floats (cut down old floats). Children hold one under each hand to begin with, then use one mini float under one hand, and, finally, they will allow the last float to slide out of the hand soon after setting off and carry on swimming without it. This is usually proof enough to the nervous child that it can swim! Setting off unsupported follows quickly.

MIDDLE GROUP

This consists of 15 lessons, which is enough work for two terms. It is necessary to teach the lessons in numerical order, but a lesson may in some cases take more than one week. At the end of each term, allow two lessons for testing.

FIRST TERM

Week 1 .... Foot check; sorting into groups and start Lesson 1.

Week 2 .... Lesson 1

Week 3 .... Lesson 2

Week 4 .... Lesson 3

Week 5 .... Lesson 4

Week 6 .... Lesson 5

Week 7 .... Lesson 6

Week 8 .... Lesson 7

Week 9 .... Testing for 25m badge and Improver's award.

Week 10 .... Testing for 25m badge and Improver's award.

This is only an approximate guide according to the ability of the children. In some instances classes may only reach Lesson 5 by week 8 whereas others could progress to Lesson 7.

SUPPLEMENTARY · ACTIVITIES

Life-saving back stroke

On pool-side seating.

(a)

Sit with legs held horizontally, as if lying flat in the water.

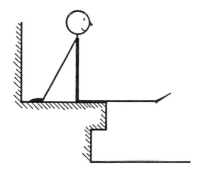 

(b)

Gently drop the lower legs – as if from the surface – knees apart. Keep tummy and thighs in line when in water.

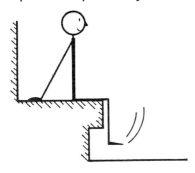 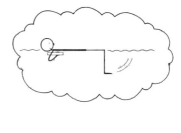

(c)

Turn feet out ('frog').

(d)
Keeping feet frogged, circle outwards and upwards and back to horizontal position.
Circle action should be strong and quick.

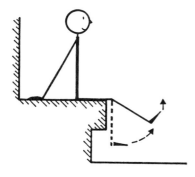

FAULTS

Toes pointed instead of frogged – weak propulsion.

Seat dropping down from surface, knees bending upwards – slow progress through water because centre of gravity (seat) is too low. This creates difficulties when towing.

MIDDLE 1

Equipment

Two floats and two armbands each on pool-side.

Life-saving back stroke dry practice first (p. 23).
Sit on pool-edge. Waist-deep area. *Number group in twos/threes.*

1 Slide feet first, back **upright**, into the water, and crouch.
Hug head down to knees and float to surface curled up.
Swimmers will slowly rise to surface; the small percentage who don't rise – sinkers – will soon stand up!
Once at surface, keep head down and count 3 seconds, i.e. 1 caterpillar, 2 caterpillar, 3 caterpillar, before lifting head. Stand up.

1 half-width **2** On tummy, with one float under each arm close to ribs, frog, push and together, and glide along, using legs only.
The last stage is a glide forwards with legs together and can only be achieved after a **strong** *push with legs.*
Keep shoulders under surface throughout. Look straight forwards throughout. *A slow-moving practice.*

3 *Repeat 2, returning to side. Make sure swimmers' legs* **are** *together during glide along.*

4 Armbands on above elbows.
Space group out, facing your side of the pool.
Start floating on tummy
in 'frog' shape.

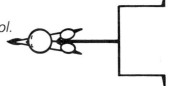

Practise changing from 'frog' into 'I' ('I' for ice) shape: legs push back, then slide together, whilst arms extend forwards until
×8 straight, palms facing down, thumbs touching.

Swimmers should finish like this.

Remove armbands.

5 Swim 2 widths *(or 4 half-widths)* breast stroke. Try to make the three shapes clearly – Y, frog, and I – especially the I.
Allow a rest only after one width (or two half-widths).

6 With a float under each arm, stand shoulder-deep.
Try to make five 'frog-push' movements with legs apart and feet frogged, and with legs pushing in a downward direction **under** body.
Keep your inside ankle bones facing the pool-floor.

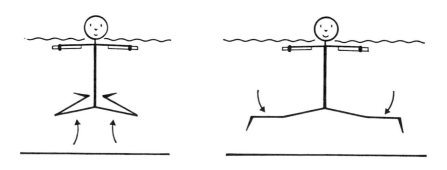

If swimmer travels forwards or backwards, legs are not under body.
Try 10 'frog-pushes'.
Try 15 'frog-pushes'.
Return to side of pool.

7 *Use armbands for any very nervous swimmers.* **Stand** facing side, a float under each arm.
Practise setting off on back correctly.

(a) Crouch, so shoulders are **under** surface.

(b) Keeping shoulders **under**, tilt head back into water.

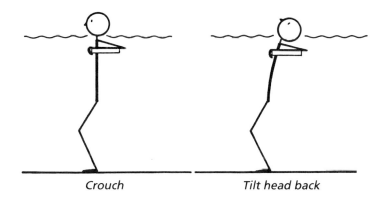

Crouch   Tilt head back

(c) With shoulders under **and** head back, push tummy up to surface. Feet will lift up off floor.

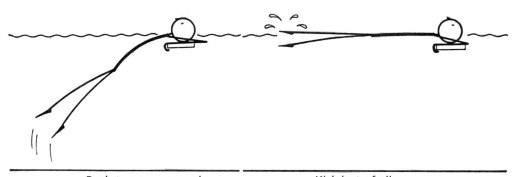

Push tummy upwards   Kick last of all

(d) Finally, kick legs gently up and down, near surface, toes pointing at pool-side.
After a few kicks, 'sit down' and bring feet back below body for standing up.
Repeat this setting off practice two or three times, then once more, beginning at pool-centre and kicking back to side.

8 (a) Space out, and try a mushroom-float – take a breath, put head right down in water and gently hug knees to chest.

(b) *If there is enough time, in twos, in a space, one partner should mushroom-float and, before lifting head, should be spun round twice by the other partner. They should then change over.*

9 Try the same again but spin your partner twice one way, then twice the other way, **before** head is raised.

MIDDLE 2

Equipment

Next week, everyone is to bring one clean, coloured sock.
Two floats and two armbands on pool-side.
Sit on pool-edge. Approximately 1m. *Number in twos/threes.*

Life-saving back stroke dry practice first (p. 23).

1 By numbers, feet first, slide into a crouch position on pool-floor. Hug head to knees and slowly mushroom-float to surface. Once at the surface, continue to float with your head down for 6 seconds before standing up.

2 With partner in a space.
One does a mushroom-float; the other spins the floater round three times before floater lifts head up. Change over.

3 *Children who are nervous on back should wear armbands.*
Practise setting off on back correctly with one float under each arm; do following sequence to achieve a good position on back.

(a) Crouch, with shoulders under surface.

(b) With shoulders under, tilt head back into water.

(c) With shoulders under and head back, push tummy up to the surface. Your feet will lift off the floor.

(d) Lastly, kick legs gently with knees under surface.

Anyone who lifts knees or feet to surface before pushing tummy up needs to repeat the setting-off sequence correctly. Practise this four times, then let group kick back to side from the centre of the pool.

4 Armbands on. In a space, facing side, float on tummy in frog shape. Practise changing into an 'I' shape, using a strong push back and together with legs, whilst extending arms forwards, ×4 thumbs together, palms down.

5 Repeat 4 but on changing into 'I' shape blow out through ×4 mouth, strongly.

6 Armbands off. Swim, non-stop, 2 widths *(or 4 half-widths)* breast stroke, remembering Y, frog, I. Blow out on every 'I' shape.

7 Hold one float in each **hand**. Stand shoulder-deep with feet flat on floor for a treading-water practice.

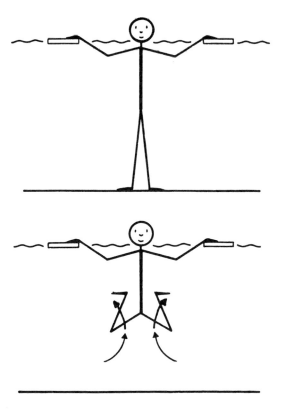

Try a frog and then push in a downward direction, keeping
×10 your feet off the floor.
×15 *Repeat after a rest.*

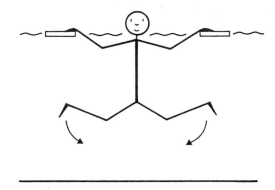

8 Stand on pool-side, toes gripping edge, feet together.
By numbers, **jump**, keeping feet together and try to land about
×2 2 metres away from pool-side.

SUPPLEMENTARY · ACTIVITIES

SUBMERGING HEAD-FIRST TO PICK UP A BRICK (OR TO TOUCH A LINE)

Waist-deep in groups of two or three.

(a) Aim at brick (or line) from about 1 metre away.

(b) Fall forwards, head down between arms.

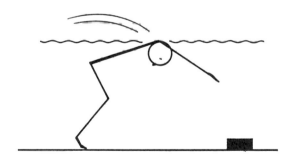

(c) Push seat upwards above surface. Grasp brick (or touch line).

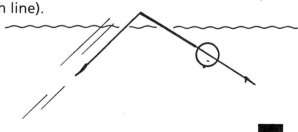

(d) Stand up, holding brick.

MIDDLE 3

Equipment

Bring a clean, coloured sock again next week.
Two floats, two armbands, and one sock on pool-side.

Sit on pool-edge. *Number group in 2s/3s.*
LSBS dry practice first (p. 23).

1 *By numbers* slide in feet first. Keep back upright until you're in a crouch. Then hug head to knees and slowly mushroom-float to surface.

2 *Nervous swimmers should try without armbands for work on back, and hold floats under arms instead of under hands.*
Setting off on back correctly. One float under each **hand**, fingers on top, elbows straight, **stand** on pool-floor.

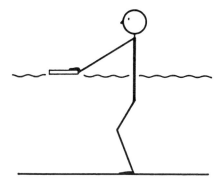

(a) Crouch so that your shoulders are under the surface.

(b) With shoulders under, tilt head back into water.

(c) With head back **and** shoulders under, push tummy up to surface. Feet will lift off floor.

(d) Finally and gently, kick legs.

Make swimmers go through these stages slowly four times, then turn around, set off once more and kick back to side.

3 Everyone with armbands on, in chest-deep water, floating on tummy in a space. Start in 'frog' shape, then push strongly into ×3 'I' shape.

Make sure that everyone has elbows tucked into sides of body, hands together and palms down, when in frog shape.

4 *Repeat 3 six more times, but with swimmers blowing out forcibly when moving into 'I' shape.*

5 Armbands off.
Swim 2 widths *(or 4 half-widths)* of breast stroke non-stop.
Make the 'I' shape after **every** frog. Blow out on every 'I' shape.

6 Take your sock from the pool-side and stand in a space with a partner.
One of the partners should hold both socks whilst mushroom-floating. Try to pass both socks under your feet to partner who is crouching behind.

Change over and let the other partner try mushroom-floating. One more turn each. Put socks on pool-side.

7 *Submerging head-first to pick up a brick or touch line on pool-floor **(see supplementary activities (p. 31)).***

8 Stand shoulder-deep, holding a float in one hand. Keeping your free hand palm down, waist-deep, draw small circles with fingertips in a vertical plane, out from body, downwards, in towards body and upwards.

Now keep the free hand circling and start both legs frog-pushing. Keep shoulders under surface.

×15

Try it with the other hand on the float, legs wide apart.

9 Try to touch the pool-floor.
×3 **(a)** With knees.
×3 **(b)** With seat.

MIDDLE 4

Equipment

Next week, bring a coloured sock.
Two armbands, two floats and one coloured sock on pool-edge.

LSBS dry practice first (p. 23).
Sit on pool-edge. *Number group in 2s/3s.*

1 *By numbers,* **feet first, slide into a crouch on the pool-floor with your back upright. Quickly bend your body down and try to touch the pool-floor with both hands 2 metres from the side. Then mushroom-float to surface.**

2 *Setting off on back correctly: no swimmers in armbands. Nervous children to work with a float under each arm, others to hold float under each hand.*
Stand up in the pool.

(a) Crouch with your shoulders under the surface.

(b) Keeping shoulders under surface, tilt head back into water.

(c) With head back and shoulders under, push tummy up to surface. Feet will lift.

(d) Finally and gently, kick legs a few kicks.

(e) Sit down (feet sink to pool floor).
Repeat this once more. All swimmers return to side.

3 *Confident swimmers using floats in hands; nervous children with floats under arms.*
All set off on back correctly and back-crawl kick across width. At centre of width, confident swimmers let floats slip from fingers, and finish width unsupported. Return and collect floats, and put them on the pool-side.

4 *Waist-deep, armbands on above elbows,* float on tummy in 'frog' shape.
Push strongly into 'I' shape blowing through mouth at same time. Whilst blowing out, tuck head between arms, nose under
×4 surface. Look **ahead**.

Return to side. Armbands off.

5 Hold trough behind with both hands, feet against wall, as you would prepare to set off from the deep end in the Improver's award. Swim 2 widths breast stroke non-stop. 'I' shape must follow **every** 'frog'. Blow out on **every** 'I' shape.

6 *Shoulder-deep.* In a space, draw small vertical circles at tummy level with both hands.

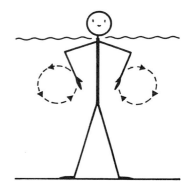

Now add one leg doing a 'frog-push' action to the hand circling.

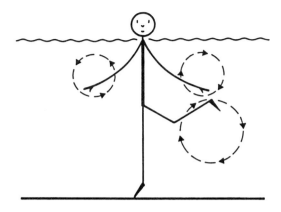

Keeping shoulders **under** surface begin frog-pushing with other leg, too. This is treading water.

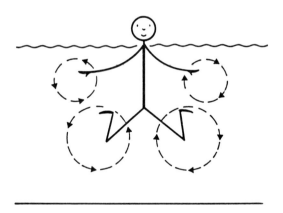

Try to do 20 frog-pushes before standing on floor.

7 *Whole group, waist-deep.*
Put on coloured sock.
Mushroom-float with eyes open and try to remove sock before
×3 lifting head and standing up.

8 *Still waist-deep,* try to swim two or three strokes along pool-
×2 floor.

MIDDLE 5

Equipment

Bring a sock next week.
2 floats and 1 coloured sock on pool-side.

Sit on pool-edge. *Number group in 2s, 3s or 4s.*
No dry LSBS practice from now on.

1 *By numbers,* **feet first, slide into a crouch (back upright) on the pool-floor, then bend body quickly forwards and try to swim along pool-floor for about 2 metres. Re-surface.**

2 *Chest-deep,* **put sock on one foot. Mushroom-float and, with eyes open, remove sock before putting feet down on pool-floor and lifting head.**

3 Hold sock in both hands, so that top is open. Now, with eyes open, mushroom-float and try to put sock on one foot, before putting feet back on floor.

4 *Submerging head-first to pick up a brick:* **see supplementary activities** *(p. 31).*

5 No one in armbands. Children nervous on back should use a float under each arm.
Practise setting off correctly on back.
Confident children to hold an **imaginary** *float in each hand.*
The sequence is: shoulders under, head back, tummy up and kick.
Kick to centre of pool then feet down, turn round, set off again and kick back to side.

6 Using a float under each arm, lie on back, with tummy, thighs and lower legs along surface.

Keeping in time with the instructions and keeping body and thighs always parallel with surface, practise life-saving back stroke. *This will be the group's first attempt at the stroke in the pool. Go slowly.*

(a) Drop lower legs, knees apart.

(b) Frog the feet.

(c) Circle lower legs forwards, outwards and up to surface with feet frogged. Repeat this slowly for 1 half-width.

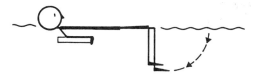

Discourage any bending at hip joint, causing hips to drop away from surface.

Return to side, using back crawl kick.

7 *Repeat 6 once more.*

8 Swim non-stop, if possible, 2 widths or 4 half-widths, breast stroke. Remember to make the 'I' shape after **every** frog. Blow out strongly during the change from frog to 'I'.

9 In shoulder-deep water, try treading water 'on the spot', for 20 frog-pushes, without putting feet on pool-floor.
Now try for 30 seconds.

MIDDLE 6

Equipment

Next week children will need an elasticated belt or piece of elastic which fits round waist. No more socks!

Two floats on pool-side, a coloured sock on.
Sit on pool-edge. *Number group in 3s/4s.*

1 Keeping back vertical, slide in feet first, into a crouch.

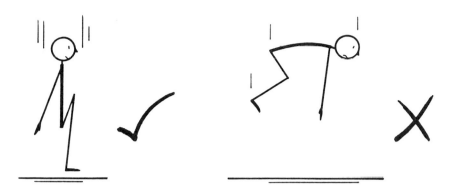

Then bend forwards quickly and try to swim **along pool-floor** for 2 metres. To stay near pool-floor, keep your head down and pull body towards floor.

2 *Try the following separately.*

(a) Mushroom-float (MF) in a space; remove sock before standing up.

(b) MF and put sock on the other foot.

(c) MF and remove sock from one foot, then put it on the other foot before coming up for air!

3 *Picking up a brick – **see supplementary activities** (p. 31).*

4 If possible, swim 2 widths or 4 half-widths breast stroke non-stop. Try not to put your feet down at all, not even when turning round or if you meet someone. Try to keep going whatever happens. Remember – blow out through mouth **every** time your hands go fowards into 'I' shape.

5 With a float under each arm, lie flat on back at surface.

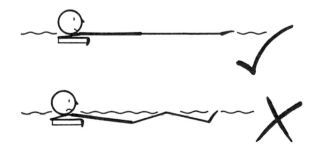

Keep body and thighs parallel with surface throughout. Following the calls, **slowly,**

(a) drop the **lower** legs, knees apart.

(b) frog your feet.

(c) keeping feet turned out, circle lower legs forwards out, and back up to surface (1 half-width).
Return to pool-side on back, using crawl kick, knees **under** surface.

6 *Repeat 5 once more. Discourage any sinking of hips away from surface.*

7 In shoulder-deep water, try treading water above the same spot for 30 frog-pushes.
*Aim for wide apart leg action and shoulders under surface. Hands must **not** lift out above surface. Feet should not touch floor until 30 pushes are completed.*

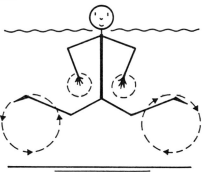

Return to places at side.

8 *Head-first surface dive: the first of four stages (second stage next week.)*
This stage is push and glide forwards.
Hold trough behind with both hands; feet up against pool-wall.

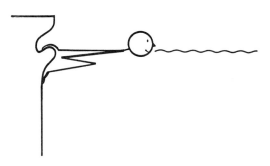

Let go. **Quickly** pass hands forwards, close to sides of body, just under surface of water.

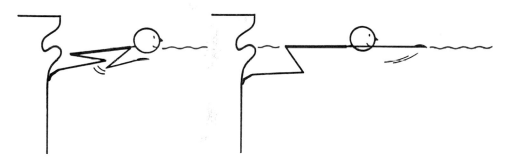

Then push off and glide forwards along surface with hands together and legs together in 'I' shape, for 2 or 3 metres – a ×3 short glide.

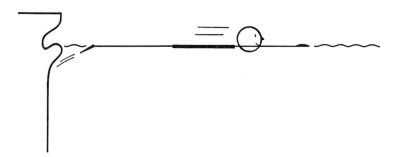

Swimmers should not fling arms over surface into the glide.

*Arms should be extended ahead **before** push-off.*

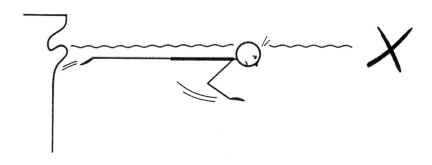

MIDDLE 7

Equipment

The children should bring elastic again next week.
Two floats on pool-side. Elastic on.

1 Sit on pool-edge, heels on trough. *Number group in 3s/4s.*
Introduction to a straddle-entry, i.e. striding in, but keeping head
above surface.
Lean forwards, arms raised ahead. Lift one leg forwards and
flop on to water, hitting arms down strongly on to surface.

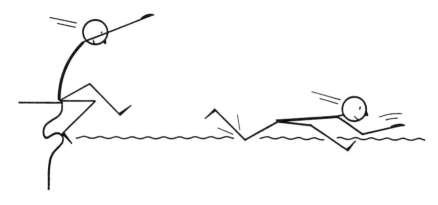

Head should not submerge at all. *This is called a 'flop' entry.*

2 Swim, in good style 2 widths or 4 half-widths breast stroke
(Y, frog, I). Each stroke must finish in 'I' shape. Blow out with
nose **under** surface on each 'I' shape. Look ahead.

3 In a space, mushroom-float and remove elastic from waist by
passing it round the thighs, round the knees, round the heels
and off the feet.
Put elastic back on and try the same practice again.
Put elastic on pool-side.

4 *LSBS practice.*

1 half-width On back, a float under each arm, body, thighs and lower legs at surface. Drop the lower legs, frog the feet and circle out, forwards and up to surface.

Return to side, kicking on back.

5 *Repeat LSBS practice, swimmers working un-directed.*

6 In shoulder-deep water, tread water above the same spot for 30 seconds and then (after a rest) for 45 seconds. Return to side.

7 Head-first surface dive (HFSD): *revision of first stage.*
Hold trough behind with both hands, feet against pool-wall.
Let go and push off and glide forwards along surface for about
×2 2 or 3 metres with arms extended ahead.

Remember **not** to lift hands and arms over surface when taking them forwards.

8 HFSD stage 2.
Repeat stage 1, then at end of short glide:
pull both arms **horizontally** right round to sides of body, hands
×3 finishing against thighs.

9 Attempt an underwater swim of three or four strokes, along pool-floor.

MIDDLE GROUP
SECOND TERM

This is a sequence of lessons that takes the children from shallow to deep water.

Week 1 .... Lesson 8

Week 2 .... Lesson 9

Week 3 .... Lesson 10

Week 4 .... Lesson 11

Week 5 .... Lesson 12

Week 6 .... Lesson 13

Week 7 .... Lesson 14

Week 8 .... Lesson 15

Week 9 .... Testing for 400m–600m badges, Intermediate and (in some cases) Proficiency.

Week 10 .... Testing for 400m–600m badges, Intermediate and (in some cases) Proficiency.

MIDDLE 8

Equipment

Next week: an elasticated belt and **clean** *pyjama or other lightweight trousers.*

Two floats on pool-side, elastic or elasticated belt on.
Sit on pool-edge. *Number group in 3s/4s.*

1 A sitting 'flop' entry *(a lead-up to straddle entry).* Use arms to hit downwards hard on to surface. Lean forwards throughout, one leg lifting ahead. Your head should not submerge.

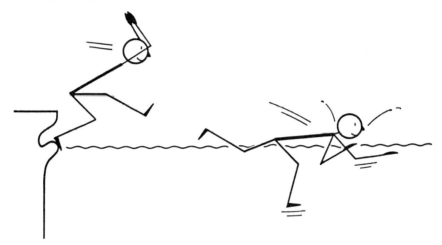

2 On back, a float under each arm, lie flat and, to instructions, practise life-saving back stroke. Drop lower legs, frog the feet, circle lower legs out, forwards and up.

3 *Repeat LSBS practice at a faster speed.*
Drop – circle, drop – circle.
Stress that the 'drop' movement is done gently and the circling is strong and fast.

4 In a space, whilst mushroom-floating, remove elastic, **then** stand up. Put elastic on again.

5 *Repeat 4,* but count 3 seconds (say in your head '1 caterpillar, 2 caterpillar, 3 caterpillar') before removing elastic.

6 In shoulder-deep water, beginning with feet flat on floor, tread water above the same spot using hands and legs for **one minute**. Every 15 seconds, do a quarter turn, to face another direction, without putting your feet down.

7 Now, tread water for 30 seconds with hands on hips.

8 In original positions at side for 1st, 2nd and 3rd stages of head-first surface dive.
Hold trough behind then:

(a) glide at surface for 2 or 3 metres.

(b) pull arms round to sides horizontally and

(c) bend body downwards from surface. Leave legs along surface with knees straight.

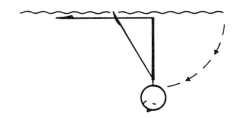

Hold this upside-down letter L position for 2 seconds, then
×3 re-surface.

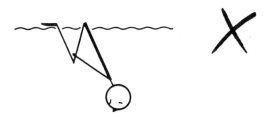

Discourage this

Knees should not bend nor hips lift above surface.
Only *the hip joint should bend to force the body down.*

9 Beginning opposite the 1 metre mark, by numbers, swim non-stop to the shallow end and back, using breast stroke. Style must be good. Blow out with nose under surface on **every 'I'** shape. Do not put feet on pool-floor once, not even when turning at shallow end, not even if you bump into someone, not even if you swallow a gallon of water suddenly!

SUPPLEMENTARY · ACTIVITIES

SAFE REMOVAL OF TROUSERS

Equipment

Pyjama or other lightweight trousers and elasticated belt or piece of elastic which fits around waist to be worn.
Explain first, then swimmers practise on pool-side.

1 Whilst treading water, remove belt by unfastening or sliding off over feet. Undo any trouser fastenings.

2 Push waistband of trousers quickly below **knees**.

3 Take a breath. Put head well down, eyes open. Mushroom-float and pull **one** trouser leg off.

4 Lift head. Take another breath. Mushroom-float and remove second trouser leg.

5 Tread water. Roll up trousers into a ball and throw out.

3 and 4 can be repeated endlessly and without panic if trousers are difficult to pull off.

MIDDLE 9

See supplementary activities above.

Equipment

Same kit next week.
Pyjama trousers and belt or elastic on. Two floats for swimmers who are still nervous when on their back.
Sit on pool-edge. *Number group in 3s/4s.*

1 A flop entry *(a basic straddle entry from sitting).* Hit hands strongly down on surface. Head should not submerge. Feet should not hit pool-floor.

2 In a space, chest-deep, mushroom-float and remove and throw belt or elastic on to pool-side.

To remove trousers: first, whilst treading water,
(a) undo button(s), then change to mushroom-floating.

(b) Thumbs inside waistband, pass waistband round seat and then round knees.

(c) Use **both hands** to free one foot. Head up, take a breath, mushroom-float.

(d) Then use **both hands** to free second foot.

Throw trousers on to pool-side. Everyone have a go.

3 Hold trough behind with both hands, feet **well up behind body** on pool-wall. Practise pushing off forwards and
×3 swimming a few strokes of breast stroke.

This is a skill needed when setting off from deep-end trough in the improver's award.

4 Using floats under arms only if nervous, set off correctly on back, kick legs up and down gently, until you are moving steadily, then change to life-saving back stroke leg action –
×2 drop-circle, drop-circle – for 1 width.

5 Shoulder-deep, tread water for 45 seconds with hands on hips.

6 *First three stages of head-first surface dive (revision).*
Hold trough behind with both hands, feet against pool-wall, glide – pull and bend. Hold 'L' shape for two seconds, eyes
×2 open, before resurfacing.

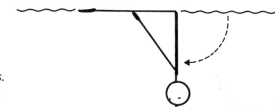

*Finish like this.
Eyes open*

7 *In slightly deeper water, keeping weaker children shallowest, practise the fourth and final stage of head-first surface dive.*
Glide – pull and bend – and **lift both legs into the air** from surface.

This leg-lift will sink swimmer to pool-floor.
Open eyes and look at pool-floor ahead. To stop body rolling over during leg lift, press hands, palms first, downwards and forwards at same time as legs lift.

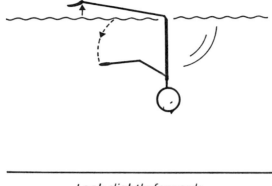

Look slightly forwards.

×3 Try to keep knees straight during leg-lift.

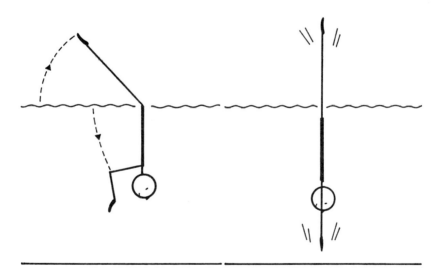

Touch the pool-floor, then re-surface.

MIDDLE 10

See Supplementary Activities (p. 47).

Equipment

Next week's kit: elastic, pyjama trousers, and long-sleeved blouse or shirt or pyjama top **buttoning right down the front.**
Pyjama trousers and elastic on. Two floats for those still nervous on back.

Sit on pool-edge. *Number group in 3s/4s.*
1 Start with a flop entry *(a simplified straddle entry).*
Swimmers should land flat on surface, but with one leg forward underneath them.
Climb out.

2 *Repeat entry, but in slightly deeper water (over 1m).*
After hitting the surface, instead of standing up, tread water for 5 seconds, swim back to shallower water (1m) and **then** stand up. Don't put feet on the pool-floor until finished completely.

3 Swim 2 half-widths breast stroke, in kit. Still try to finish each stroke with a glide (letter 'I'). Turn round at pool-centre without putting feet on floor.

4 *In chest-deep water.*
Whilst mushroom-floating, remove elastic or belt first and, after a short rest, mushroom-float again and remove trousers. Remember to free feet one at a time. Put kit on pool-side.

5 Use floats under arms **only** if unable to swim on back.
Set off correctly, *i.e. shoulders under, head back,* **tummy** *up and kick, then* change to life-saving back stroke once moving on back (2 half-widths).
Swimmers who are competent on back should set off using life-saving back stroke and try to do 2 half-widths, non-stop.

6 Hold trough behind with both hands, feet up behind body on pool-wall.

×2 Glide – pull and bend *(bend at hip joint),* opening your eyes under water. Hold for two seconds, then stand up.

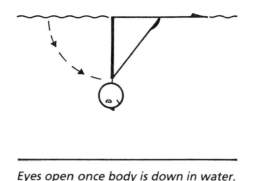

Eyes open once body is down in water.

7 *Move group shoulder-deep, apart from any nervous swimmers who should stay in 1m depth.*
Practise final stage of head-first surface dive.
Glide – pull and bend – and lift both legs from surface into air.
During leg lift, stop your body rolling over by pressing your hands and arms down, then forwards, strongly.
Try to keep knees straight and legs together during the lift.
×2 Eyes should be open once your body is down in water. Look slightly ahead.

8 Return to original places. On your back, hug one float above chest with your right arm. Trail the left hand in water, close to left thigh.

Back-crawl kick: even kicking at surface. Count kicks in threes:
2 half- 1, 2, 3, 1, 2, 3, 1, 2, 3, and so on.
widths Kick at your own preferred speed.

9 *Repeat* with the left arm holding float and the right hand trailing close to thigh.

MIDDLE 11

See supplementary activities (p. 47).

Equipment

No kit next week and until further notice.
Kit on: trousers, elastic, long-sleeved, button-down-the-front top.
T-shirts will not do – leave them off. Two floats for those still lacking confidence when on back.

1 Sit on pool-edge around 1 metre mark. Without putting feet on pool-floor do a flop entry and swim 2 widths breast stroke.

2 Shoulder-deep, tread water and remove top – undo buttons, peel top back off shoulders. With arms behind back, pull one sleeve off. Remove second sleeve. Wrap top in a tight ball and throw out. Put feet down and have a short rest.

3 Mushroom-float and remove elastic. Short rest, then mushroom-float again and remove trousers.
Free feet one at a time. Put kit on pool-side. Return to original places at 1 metre depth.

4 Swim 2 widths life-saving back stroke without stopping.

5 Shoulder-deep, tread water using arms and legs for one minute and 15 seconds.

Note – Notify lifeguard of following situation:

On their own, in shallow water, using a work sheet devised by the teacher, will be swimmers who:
(a) *cannot mushroom-float with confidence, and/or*

(b) *cannot swim on back, unsupported, and/or*

(c) *cannot tread water for 30 seconds without a struggle.*

The remainder should climb out. After impressing on them the need for **absolute co-operation**, *take them to 1.8m to begin introductory deep water practices.*
Remind these children to follow instructions precisely. Working in deep water may be a totally new experience to some of the group, so **no risks** *must be taken by anyone.*

Introductory deep water practices for the middle group members who are technically competent

1.8m water depth. * *Keep nervous children together at one end of group. By safest means establish group in water, holding trough or rail. Insist that no one lets go until told to. For the safety of the group, anyone who is not prepared to follow instructions must return to shallow water to work. Number in 2s/3s.*

×3 **6** Hold on with both hands. **Do not let go at all.** Keeping body and legs against wall of pool, push both arms straight and try to touch the floor with your toes. Pull back up to surface.

×2 **7** Repeat previous activity but, when arms are at full stretch, open your eyes and look up. Try to see lights on ceiling. Pull up with one hand on the trough and the other hand pulling downwards through the water. **Eyes open immediately on re-surfacing.**

×3 **8** This time, as your head re-surfaces, start treading water with your legs and the free arm (5 seconds). Still keep one hand on trough throughout.

9 By numbers, keeping one hand on trough, tread water using both legs and one arm, shoulders under surface. At the word 'go', slide hand from trough into water, continue treading water for 5 seconds then take hold of trough again.

10 *Repeat but tread water for 10 seconds without holding trough.*

11 Push down to stand on pool-floor. Let go with both hands. Pull through water to surface. As head re-surfaces, tread water 5 seconds, then hold trough. Eyes open immediately on re-surfacing.

12 Drop from trough, arms above head. Land with feet on pool-floor. Pull to surface. Tread water for 10 seconds. Hold trough.

13 Facing trough, tread water for 5 seconds. Then turn and tread water with your back to the trough for 5 seconds.

14 *Repeat, but treading water for 15 seconds facing in each direction.*

* Don't go too deep. The pool-floor should be only a couple of inches beyond reach of the smaller children, with their arms at full stretch. Being able to touch the floor and to return quickly to the surface increases confidence.

15 Sit on pool-edge, with your heels on the trough. Lean forwards and flop on to surface. Tread water for 5 seconds. Turn and swim to trough.

MIDDLE 12

Equipment

No extra kit until further notice.
One float only, if confident when swimming on back. If still nervous on back, two floats.

1 Sit on pool-edge, with your heels on trough (1m depth). By numbers, do a flop entry. Make a good smacking sound on surface with your arms.

2 Swim 4 widths breast stroke without stopping. *Correct any careless work instantly. Point out that only those capable of maintaining a good style will be suitable for the deep end group.*

3 Non-stop, swim 2 widths life-saving back stroke. Try to do the first width with hands on hips.
Correct any tendency in the swimmers to raise their knees above the surface.
Lower legs should be dropped from and circled back to the surface.

4 Still on your back, hug one float above your chest in your right arm. Back-crawl kick, counting kicks in threes (1, 2, 3, 1, 2, 3, 1, 2, 3, and so on). Kick evenly and at a speed which is comfortable. Lift your left arm to point at the ceiling on 1, 2, 3, and then return it to the side of your body by the same route on the next 1, 2, 3, and so on, across width. Keep your left arm straight.

5 Repeat using your left arm to hold the float and your right arm to lift and lower. Kick strongly.

6 Chin-deep, tread water for one minute with one hand on the opposite shoulder.

Divide group: weaker swimmers should work from special scheme displayed on pool-side. Others should move to deep end, with usual reminders about co-operation (see note on p. 52).

Introductory deep water practices

(1.8m–2m) water depth.
Hold trough with both hands. *Number group in 2s/3s.*

×2 **7** Keeping hold with both hands and with your body close to wall, push down until your arms are at full stretch. Open eyes and look at person next to you and smile. Then count to three slowly. Pull up again.

×2 **8** Take a breath and 'drop' off the trough, arms up above head. **Open your eyes**. Return to the surface, pulling down through the water with both arms. Hold the trough.

9 Tread water using both arms and legs, keeping shoulders under surface and using symmetrical, wide apart leg action.
(a) 5 seconds and hold trough again.
(b) 10 seconds and hold trough again.
(c) 15 seconds and hold trough again.

10 Hold trough behind with both hands, feet well up against wall.

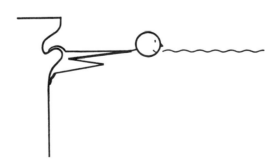

Let go, push off and swim forwards three breast strokes, turn and swim back towards trough. When 1 metre from trough, tread water for 3 seconds, then complete swim to trough.

11 Begin as before, and swim three breast strokes forwards. Turn, tread water for 3 seconds, then swim to trough.

12 Face and hold the trough, with your feet against the wall.

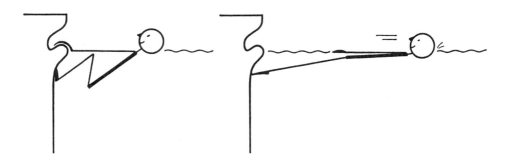

Let go. **Gently** push tummy to surface, then swim three life-saving back strokes. Change to treading water for 3 seconds. Swim back to trough, breast stroke.

13 Sit on pool-edge. Lean forwards. Flop in. Tread water for 5 seconds. Turn and swim back. Climb out.
Explain that leaning forward on entry prevents swimmer sinking too deep.

14 Stand on pool-side, gripping the edge with toes of both feet. Lean forwards. Jump in with body leaning forwards and legs slightly apart. Tread water for 5 seconds. Swim back and climb out.

15 Stand on edge. Grip edge with toes. Jump in with body upright and, legs together, **go down to pool-floor**. Push from the floor with your feet and pull up using your arms against the ×3 water. Tread water for 5 seconds. Turn and climb out.

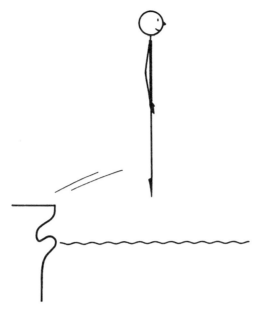

Swimmers who lean forwards will not sink to the pool-floor.

MIDDLE 13

Equipment

One float each (two floats if still lacking confidence on back).

1 Stand on pool-edge *around the 1 metre mark*, **grip** edge with toes of **both** feet. Jump fowards, keeping feet together. Try to jump 2 metres (if lines are marked, land on line 2) feet first. **No dives.**

×2 **2** Sit on pool-floor whilst counting 4 seconds.

3 Swim 4 widths non-stop. On widths 1 and 4 use life-saving back stroke; on widths 2 and 3 use breast stroke. No feet down on pool-floor at any time.

4 On your back, hold float above chest with your right arm. Crawl kick evenly, big toes leaving a foamy trail on surface. Count kicks in threes. On the first 1, 2, 3, lift your left arm up, little finger side of hand leading, and over to touch surface beyond your left shoulder.

On the next 1, 2, 3, return your left arm to the side of your body by the same route, i.e. over through air, and so on.
Keep the elbow straight.

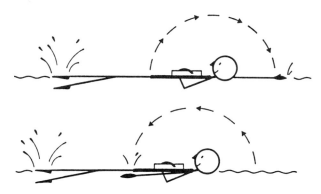

1 width This is hard work. Your legs must kick strongly.

5 Repeat using the other arm.

Divide the group as for the previous two lessons (see p. 52).

Introductory deep water practices

6 Swim to the trough *at 1.8m–2m depth* using breast stroke.

7 Hold the trough with both hands. Push up on hands quickly to get some height above surface, then drop, raising arms above head, legs together, body upright. Sink to the floor, then
×2 push up, and tread water for 10 seconds. Hold trough.

8 *Begin as before* and sink to the floor. Push up and re-surface, and immediately sink to floor again. Push up. Tread water for 10 seconds, then hold trough.

9 One after another, swim breast stroke across the deep end, touch the wall, then turn and swim back, following a circuit.

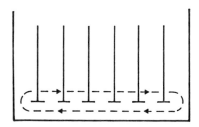
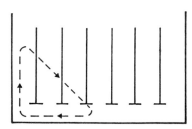

Tread water on the call 'stop', continue swimming on the call 'go'.
Keep going for 1 minute and 15 seconds altogether, unless swimmers begin to tire sooner.
Rest at trough when finished.

10 Hold trough behind with both hands. Push off and swim three breast strokes forwards. Turn to face trough and tread water. Lift both arms above head, slide legs together and sink to floor feet-first. Push up. Tread water for 5 seconds. Return to side, and climb out.

11 Stand gripping edge with toes. Jump in, keeping your body upright, legs together. Sink to floor, **then crouch**. Push to surface. Tread water for 10 seconds, swim to side and climb out.

12 Repeat previous activity but, once in crouch, hug head to knees and mushroom-float to surface. This re-surfacing will be slow. Tread water for 10 seconds. Swim to side and climb out.

13 *A basic sitting dive:* sit about 15 centimetres back from pool-edge, heels on trough. With arms straight and hands together, palms down, aim fingers **forwards** and downwards, as if down a slide. With **head down between arms**, slide down into water fingers first. Keep arms **in front** of head
×3 whilst going downwards. Turn fingers upwards to re-surface.

MIDDLE 14

Equipment

One float each (two if still lacking confidence when on back).

1 Stand on pool-edge around the 1-metre mark *(or as appropriate so the children will be shoulder deep)*. Grip edge with toes. Jump **forwards** about 2 metres. **After** take-off, and in the air, turn to land in pool facing the side.

2 Submerge and touch pool-floor with seat and then knees
×2 before re-surfacing.

3 Swim non-stop for 4 widths. Start each width using breast stroke, but at the centre of each width change to life-saving back stroke. Your feet must not touch the floor at any time during these four widths.

4 On your back, hold one float above chest in right hand. Back-crawl kick at surface evenly, and strongly. Count kicks in threes.
On first 1, 2, 3, lift left arm up, little finger side of hand leading, over to touch surface ahead of left shoulder.
On next 1, 2, 3, return left arm by the same route, over through 1 width air, to left side. Keep elbow straight. Continue across the pool.

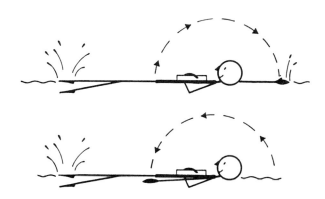

5 Return using the other arm.

6 On your back, still kicking and counting as before, with your right arm holding the float above your chest.
On first 1, 2, 3, lift left arm over and into water, little finger side of hand first.
On your next 1, 2, 3, keeping elbow straight, sweep arm **horizontally** through water, just under surface to left side. Continue for one width. Keep thumb of pulling hand (left) uppermost during horizontal sweep through water.
Repeat, using other arm.
The following activities should be attempted shoulder-deep by all swimmers who have not done deep-water practices during the last three lessons (Middle 11, 12 and 13), and in 2m water by the stronger section of the group.

7 Head-first surface dive starting at trough, i.e. glide – pull and ×2 bend – and lift.

8 Tread water for 1 minute 30 seconds.

9 Jump in with legs together and back upright. Sink into a ×2 crouch. Hug head to knees and mushroom-float to surface.

MIDDLE 15

Equipment

One float each.
Stand on pool-edge (1m).

1 Jump in, keeping back **upright** and feet together. Sink to pool-floor into crouch. Then hug head down to knees and mushroom-float to surface.
*When everyone has done this, explain that this **sinking** action is the same as a feet-first surface dive.*
Climb out.

2 Repeat, but after re-surfacing, swim two widths life-saving back stroke and two widths breast stroke, non-stop. Feet should not touch the floor between re-surfacing and swimming.

3 On your back, one float held above chest in right arm, back-crawl kick, counting kicks in 3s.
On your first 1, 2, 3, lift left arm, elbow straight, up and over to surface ahead of left shoulder.
On your next 1, 2, 3, left arm should enter water, little finger first, and sweep to left thigh **horizontally** just under surface, 1 width elbow straight and thumb uppermost throughout sweep.

4 Repeat using right arm.

5 On back, no float, back-crawl kick. Lift your arms over and 2 sweep **alternately**. Keep counting. During one arm's sweep, separate the other arm should lift over. Try to brush your ear with the widths lifting arm. Do not allow head to turn from side to side.

6 Move to deep water (*1.8m maximum*) only those safe in deep water. Hold trough. Practise a sequence of treading water (TW) and mushroom-floating (MF) in preparation for removal of clothing in water.
TW for 5 seconds
MF for 5 seconds
TW for 4 seconds
MF for 4 seconds
and so on, down to 1 second.

7 At side of deep end, hold trough behind with both hands, feet on pool-wall. Glide – pull and bend – and lift (head-first surface dive), legs together throughout. On reaching pool-floor, with **eyes open** swim two or three strokes forwards with tummy close to floor. Then re-surface.

8 Repeat, but try three or four strokes along pool-floor.

9 Back to 1 metre depth.
On your tummy, hold one float under chest with both arms.
Front-crawl kick at the surface. Kick evenly. Leave a foamy trail.
2 widths Count kicks in 3s.

Make sure toes are pointing backwards and not downwards.

Knees straight   *Move legs at
                                      hip joints*

MIDDLE GROUP
THIRD TERM

PROGRESSING TO DEEP GROUP WORK

At the beginning of this term some re-grouping will be needed to enable the stronger middle group swimmers to progress to work in deep water. The remaining swimmers can repeat middle group work by combining with shallow group children who have progressed to this level.

Week 1 .... Deep Lesson 1

Week 2 .... Deep Lesson 2

Week 3 .... Deep Lesson 3

Week 4 .... Deep Lesson 4

Week 5 .... Deep Lesson 5

Week 6 .... Deep Lesson 6

Week 7 .... Deep Lesson 7

Week 8 .... Deep Lesson 8

Week 9 .... Testing of Proficiency, Bronze Survival, 1000m badge and 1500m badge.

Week 10 .... Testing of Proficiency, Bronze Survival, 1000m badge and 1500m badge.

Note *In pools where there is a great depth of water it is advisable for teaching purposes to choose an area not more than 2m deep, or to limit descent to a swimmer's own height with arms extended above the head.*

DEEP GROUP · FIRST TERM

This consists of a series of 24 lessons designed to lead up to the Swimming Teachers' Association Survival Award Scheme, distance swimming and Proficiency and Advanced awards.

Week 1 .... Introductory Deep lesson

Week 2 .... Lesson 1

Week 3 .... Lesson 2

Week 4 .... Lesson 3

Week 5 .... Lesson 4

Week 6 .... Lesson 5

Week 7 .... Lesson 6

Week 8 .... Lesson 7

Week 9 .... Lesson 8

Week 10 .... Lesson 9

Week 11 .... Testing: Proficiency and Advanced, STA Survival and Distance.

Week 12 .... Testing: Proficiency and Advanced, STA Survival and Distance.

FRONT CRAWL PRACTICES

Application failure

1 Ar ...... hold one float ahead in your right ha... ...eping your right arm straight. Kick legs. Your left arm sho... ...eat the f...........:

(a) ...to water, fingertips ...st, forward under float...

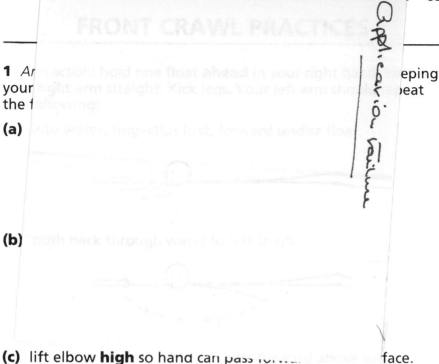

(b) push back through water to left thigh.

(c) lift elbow **high** so hand can pass .... above ...face.

1 width **Elbow should always be higher than hand.**
Repeat for the other arm.

2 *Crawl kick:* on tummy, hold one float in both arms under chest.

Toes pointing backwards, feet ruffling surface, kick evenly at your own preferred speed. Move legs from hips.
1 width Count the kicks: 1, 2, 3, 1, 2, 3, 1, 2, 3, and so on.

3 An easy introduction to breathing and blowing: hold your float as in the last practice. Kick and count kicks in threes.
1, 2, 3, head up. Breathe in.

1 width 1, 2, 3, dip head, nose under. Blow out. And so on.

4 Correct breathing and blowing: hold float as before. Count kicks in threes.
1, 2, 3, turn head to side. Breathe in.

1, 2, 3, turn head to look forward, eyebrows at surface. Blow out.

1 or 2
widths And so on. Always turn head to same side.

5 Next, add an arm pull on the breathing side. Hold one float ahead in both hands. Count kicks in threes. For example,

1, 2, 3, turn head to left.
    Pull with left arm and return it to the float.
    Breathe in as elbow lifts.

1, 2, 3, look forward. Eyebrows level with surface.
    Keep both hands on float.
    Blow out. And so on.

1 or 2
widths Turn the head to the left to breathe in throughout practice.

6 Now add an arm pull on the blow **and** on the breathe. Hold the float ahead in both hands. Count kicks in threes. For example,

1, 2, 3, turn head to left.
> Pull with left arm and return it to float.
> Breathe in as the elbow lifts.

1, 2, 3, head **forwards**.
> Pull with other arm and return your hand to the float.
> Blow out as right elbow lifts.

And repeat this sequence across the pool. Turn left to breathe in throughout practice.

7 Without float, try front crawl. Breathe to preferred side.

INTRODUCTORY DEEP LESSON

Equipment

Clean lightweight or pyjama trousers and a piece of elastic to go round waist next week.
One float on pool-edge.

1 Stand, gripping pool-edge with toes, feet together. Keep back vertical and jump in. Sink feet-first to pool-floor. Crouch, then push to surface strongly and fast.

2 On tummy hold one float ahead in **both** hands; keep elbows straight, shoulders under surface the whole time, and practise 'frog, push and together, and float along' *(legs together, knees straight)* for four widths non-stop. *This is a slow practice.*

3 Do two widths breast stroke non-stop. End each stroke with a glide.

Try to do width 1 (12m distance) in ten strokes only; width 2 in eight strokes only.

4 In a space in deep water, mushroom-float keeping your head down for about 15 seconds.

Recite the whole of 'Three Blind Mice' or 'Humpty Dumpty' with head down. Or count caterpillars!

5 *First stage head-first surface dive or do a complete head-first surface dive if the swimmers have been working at this skill recently in the middle group.*
Hold trough behind, feet against pool-wall.

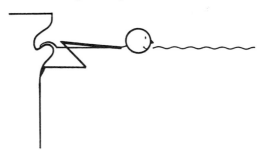

Let go. Quickly stretch arms ahead, passing them close to sides of body, just under surface. Push off strongly and glide forwards 3 metres along surface (a short glide). Keep legs pressed tightly together, knees straight, and toes pointed
×3 during the glide.

6 Using life-saving back stroke and hands sculling by thighs, do the following strengthening practice. Start in water, facing side and holding trough with both hands.

Push off. Swim across width.
Climb out. Walk to touch wall; back to pool edge and jump in.

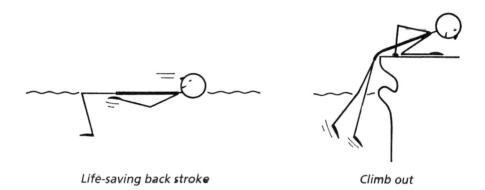

Life-saving back stroke

Climb out

Walk to wall . . .

. . . and back

Jump in

Repeat the swim, climb out, touch wall and jump in, three more times without a rest.

7 *Front crawl practice 2 (see p. 65).*

8 *Front crawl practice 3 (see p. 65).*

9 Sit on deep-end edge (1.8–2m), heels on trough, hands with thumbs together, elbows straight, head down between arms. Point fingers forwards and down.

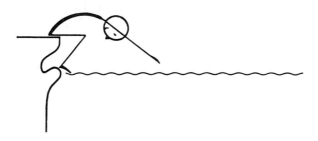

×3   Keep hands together and **in front** of head and slide down towards a spot 2 metres from pool-side. Re-surface.

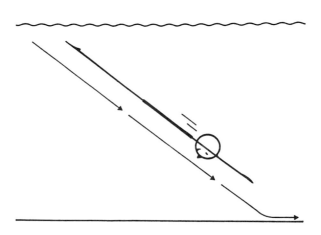

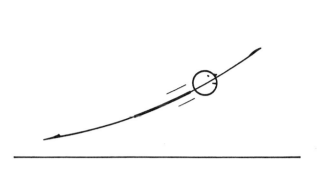

DEEP 1

Equipment

Elastic and trousers again next week.
One float on pool-side, survival practice kit on.

Number group in 2s/3s.

1 On pool-side practise safe removal of trousers (p. 47).
Put trousers on again and stand on pool-edge.

2 By numbers lean body forwards and make a straddle entry into pool.
Keep body leaning forwards throughout the entry. Head should **not** submerge.

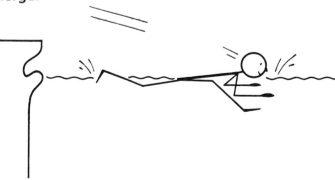

3 In kit, swim **non-stop** 4 widths life-saving back stroke. Keep up a steady pace — do **not** slow down. No collisions when turning at trough.

4 Holders of any STA survival award go to 2-metre deep water; others to chin-deep water. Mushroom-float and keep head down until each toe on right foot has been pinched by left hand and vice versa.

5 Repeat, but this time each hand must pinch each toe on both feet. Open eyes to look at toes. Climb out.
Remove practice kit on pool-side. Feet first, slide back into pool. Hold trough.

6 *Front crawl practice 1 (p. 65).*

7 *Front crawl practice 3 (p. 65).*

8 *First stage of head-first surface dive (middles progressing on to deep work do complete dive).*
Hold trough behind you, feet against wall. Pass hands forwards by a quick bending of elbows and then a straightening of arms ahead. With hands together, palms down, push off and glide
×3 forwards along surface for 3 metres (a short glide).

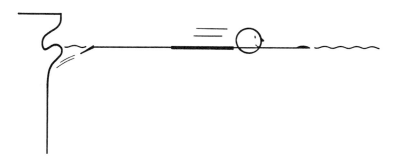

Hands must not be lifted over surface.
Keep legs together, knees straight, toes pointed.

DEEP 2

Equipment

Next week, trousers and elastic or elasticated belt.
One float on pool-side, survival kit on.

1 On pool-side, quickly practise **safe** removal of trousers (p. 47). Put trousers on again and stand on pool-edge.

2 Straddle entry into pool. Lean body forwards before striding off edge and keep body leaning forwards throughout the entry.

Keep your head up. Head should not submerge.

3 In kit, non-stop, 2 widths life-saving back stroke with hands on hips. No collisions when turning at trough – look back before setting off.

4 Everyone to chin-deep water. Mushroom-float with eyes open and fingers linked behind knees. Pass feet back over linked hands one at a time, then forward again, before lifting head.

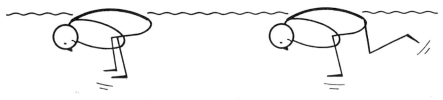

5 *Give a brief reminder about removing trousers safely (p. 47).* Then everyone should try to do it without putting their feet down on pool-floor at all. Roll up kit and throw it out.

6 *Front crawl practice 1 (p. 65).*

7 *Front crawl practice 3 (p. 65).*

8 *Front crawl practice 4 (p. 66). Only turn* **left** *to breathe in.*

9 Hold one float in both hands. Float upright. Do 2 widths non-stop of 'frog, push and together and float along'. Keep shoulders under the surface all the time.

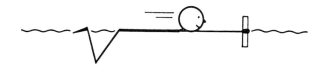

Each 'float along' should have legs together and knees straight and should last about 1 metre.

10 Sit on deep-end edge, heels on trough, hands with thumbs together, pointing to a spot on floor approximately 2 metres from side.
Head down between arms, slide, finger tips first, **keeping head between arms** all the time, down towards pool-floor. Then ×3 turn hands up to re-surface.

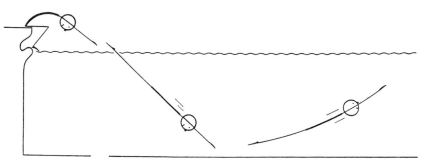

Remind the swimmers that for safety, entry is always **forwards** and downwards, not straight down.

DEEP 3

Equipment

Next week, T-shirt and usual elasticated belt and trousers.
One float on pool-side. Survival kit on.

1 *A brief reminder about removing trousers safely (p. 47).*

2 Stand on pool-edge. Lean forwards and make a straddle entry into water. Try to stride at least 1 metre.

3 Swim 4 widths life-saving back stroke non-stop. On widths 3 and 4, lift hands above surface. No collisions!

4 Survival award holders to 2-metre deep water; others to chin-deep water.
All remove trousers whilst treading water. Once trousers are off, continue to tread water, until everyone is holding trousers, rolled up, above the surface. Then throw your trousers out, without touching pool-side or floor. Swim to side. Climb out without using trough.
Remove any remaining kit. Slide feet first into pool – original places.

5 *Front crawl practice 1 (p. 65).*

6 *Front crawl practice 4 (p. 66). Turning left to breathe in.*

7 *First and second stages of head-first surface dive:* hold trough behind with both hands, feet against pool-wall. Let go, pass hands ahead, push off and glide along surface for 3 metres. Then pull both arms **outwards** and round to sides of body,
×4 **horizontally**. Glide – and pull.

8 Non-stop, swim 4 widths of a smooth breast stroke. By holding the glide ('I' shape) each time, try to use no more than seven strokes per width (12 m).

9 From deep-end edge, do a slide dive.
Start in sitting position with heels on trough. Aim fingertips forwards and downwards. Keep head between arms until re-surfacing. Keep arms **in front** of head whilst going towards
×2 floor.

SUPPLEMENTARY · ACTIVITIES

SAFE REMOVAL OF TOP (T-shirt or vest) – OVER HEAD

1 Cross your arms over in front of your body.

2 Grasp the hem of your top, reaching round towards back.

3 Wriggle the hem up to shoulders.

4 With right hand, pull hem forwards over left shoulder, down left arm and over elbow. Release left hand.

5 Use left hand to release right in the same way.

6 When both arms are free, push both thumbs up inside neck of top, gathering garment up in your hands.

7 Lift garment cleanly over head, keeping the neck of the top stretched open.

DEEP 4

Equipment

Next week, T-shirt, trousers and elastic.
One float on pool-side. Kit on.

1 On pool-side, practise safe removal of top which has to come off **over** head.
Then put top on again and stand on pool-edge.

2 Straddle entry. Use arms strongly, striking them down hard on to surface. Aim to enter 2 metres from side, at least.

3 In kit, swim 6 widths non-stop on back. On widths 1 and 2, do back-crawl kick only, with one float held above head in both hands.

Widths 3 and 4, do life-saving back stroke (LSBS) using hands in water to push.
Widths 5 and 6, LSBS with forearms out of water.

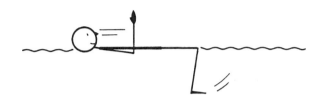

4 All in chin-deep water. Remove correctly, and throw out on to pool-side, trousers and then top, without putting feet down on floor or touching side with hands. Tread water until everyone has thrown out all kit. Then swim to deep end and, without using trough or rail, climb out.

5 Slide back into pool, at the point where the lesson began. First and second stages of a head-first surface dive (HFSD). Hold trough behind with both hands, feet against pool-wall. Let go, pass hands forward. Push off and glide along surface for 3 metres, then pull both arms **outwards** and round to sides of
×2 body horizontally, i.e. glide – and pull.

6 *First three stages of HFSD.*
Glide – and pull, and then bend body down vertically from surface by flexing hips. Eyes open, please: look at the floor
×3 slightly ahead.

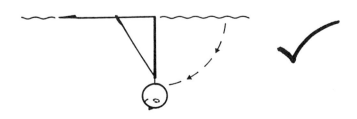

Do not allow knees to bend or legs to drop down.

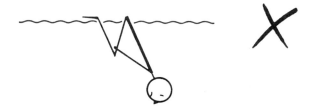

Hold correct position for 2 seconds, then re-surface.

7 *Front crawl practice 4 (p. 66). Turning head* **right** *to breathe.*

8 Sit on pool-edge at 2 metres depth, heels on trough. Imagine being at the top of a slide, the bottom of which rests on the floor 2 metres from side. Fingertips first and with head **between arms**, go down towards the bottom of slide, then re-surface. To protect head, keep hands and arms in front of
×3 head whilst going downwards.

9 Swim as fast as possible. Try to do 4 widths (48m) breast stroke in under a minute.

DEEP 5

Equipment

Next week, trousers and elastic.
One float on pool-side. Practice kit on.

1 On pool-side, practise safe removal of top over head (p. 76). Replace it, then stand on pool-edge.

2 Straddle entry landing 2 metres from side (if possible). Then, non-stop, 4 widths back crawl kick only. On first and second widths, keep forearms above surface. On widths 3 and 4 place hands on opposite shoulders.

3 To deep water, the following:

(a) *holders of any survival award.*

(b) *non-holders you know to be competent in removing trousers. Other swimmers – chin-deep. If unknown, leave chin-deep.*

All tread water for 1 minute. Then, immediately, without putting feet on floor or resting at trough, remove trousers, elastic and top (if worn) and throw them out. Swim to nearest

side and climb out without using trough.
Slide back into pool where lesson began.

4 Hold trough behind with both hands, feet against pool-wall.
First two stages **only** of head-first surface dive: glide (on
×1 surface) – and pull (both arms **horizontally** round to sides).

5 *First three stages of HFSD:*
×2 glide – pull – and bend hips.

Hold for 2 seconds before returning to trough.

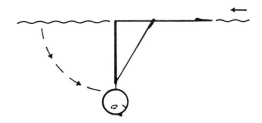

6 *Starting as in 5.*
Add the final movement to produce the complete HFSD. Once
body has been pushed down into vertical, lift both legs from
surface into the air, above your body. This sinks you to the
pool-floor. As lift begins, press palms of hands downwards, then
forwards, to keep body in vertical position.

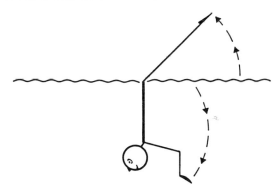

Glide – pull and bend – and lift. Touch floor then push back
×3 to surface.

7 *Front crawl practice 4 (p. 66) turning head* **right** *to
breathe in.*

8 Sit on pool-edge, heels on trough at deep end (1.8–2m

depth). One 'down-a-slide' dive, towards pool-floor 2 metres from side. Keep head between arms whilst going down.

9 *Starting as in 8.* Imagine passing **over** a hump-backed bridge before going down the slide. Arms and head slide down far side of bridge, knees straighten to lift seat over the top of the bridge.
Stress forward aspect of whole movement.

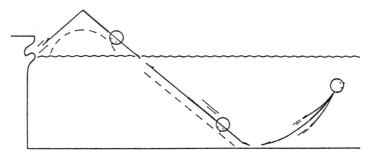

×3 Keep arms ahead until re-surfacing.

10 Finish with 4 widths (48m) breast stroke in under 1 minute.

S U P P L E M E N T A R Y · A C T I V I T I E S

FLOAT-MAKING

1 Having removed trousers, first make sure both trouser legs are the same way out, then fasten zips or buttons.

2 Tie a large, loose knot in one trouser leg. Work the knot to the ankle end and then tighten it. This is easier than tying a knot right at the end of the leg.

3 Repeat process with the other trouser leg.

4 Spread trousers on the water surface with the fly-opening, if there is one, uppermost. Encircle waist end of trousers with **one** hand (two hands cannot close up the entrance tightly enough to keep air in). Hold around lower end of any fly-opening.

5 Make sure there **is** an air passage through waist by pushing a finger through first, then blow air in until both legs are inflated. Tighten the hand holding the float to stop air escaping. Don't tie air passage in a knot in case re-inflation is needed. Hold the end closed or twist it.

6 When in the water, lie back and hold the float above your thighs. Lift your body up to the float; don't pull float down under surface.
If swimmers are finding this difficult, you could suggest they practise float-making in the bath at home!

DEEP 6

Equipment

Next week Gold and Merit swimmers should bring a long-sleeved top, e.g. a sweater; Silvers and Bronzes should bring T-shirts. All should bring trousers and elastic.
One float (polystyrene) on pool-edge.

A pool-side practice of float-making for entire group.
Then, wearing trousers and belts/elastic (no tops):

1 Straddle entry. Land 2 metres from side. Non-stop, swim 4 widths back crawl, using arms **and** legs, and 4 widths breast stroke.

2 Survival award holders and competent non-holders go to 2-metres-deep water – others chin-deep. All remove trousers and throw **belts** only on to pool-side, without standing on floor or touching the side.

3 Gold and Silver survival holders stay at deep end. Make a float in no more than 30 seconds, then float with it for 1 minute.
Others, chin-deep, try to make a float whilst treading water.

4 *Front crawl. The decision time: having experienced breathing on the left, then on the right, swimmers must choose which side they prefer.*
Then do front crawl practice 5 (p. 66) breathing on preferred side.

5 Hold trough behind, then do a complete head-first surface dive: glide – pull (arms) and bend (hips) – and lift (legs off surface).
Remind swimmers to press hands forwards and downwards as legs are lifted from surface.
×2 Keep your legs together throughout.

6 Between 1.8 and 2m, surface dive from holding the trough as before but once on pool-floor, swim three, four or five strokes
×2 forwards along floor. Then re-surface.

7 At 2m depth sit on edge, heels on trough, head between arms, arms pointing over top of imaginary hump-back bridge.

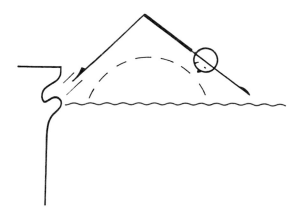

Slide over far side of bridge, pushing seat upwards slightly. Then, still with head between arms, continue down and ×2 **forwards** towards pool-floor. Re-surface.

DEEP 7

Equipment

Next week, same kit, i.e. trousers, belts/elastic, and long-sleeved sweater for Golds and Merits; T-shirts for Bronzes and Silvers. One float on pool-side. Survival practice kit on.

1 Straddle entry. Land 2 metres from side.

2 Swim 6 widths breast stroke non-stop. Keep up a constant speed. By holding the 'I' or glide position at end of each stroke, try to do each width (12m) in no more than 10 strokes.

3 *Survival award holders and competent non-holders to deep end; others chin-deep.*
All tread water for one minute, 'shielding your eyes from the sun' with one hand. Then continue for one more minute. Golds and Merits wave both arms above your head, Bronzes and Silvers use arms and legs normally.
When you have finished, hold the trough or stand chin-deep.

4 In same area and whilst treading water, remove top, elastic and trousers. Throw out top and elastic. Make a float with trousers (p. 81). *Remind group to make sure that both trouser legs are same way out, before any knots are tied. Allow 1 minute only,* *from the last swimmer beginning a float.* **Throw floats out. Return to original places.**

5 *Front crawl practice 5 (p. 66) breathing on preferred side.*

6 Between 1.8 and 2m, head-first surface dive from trough: glide – pull and bend – and lift. Remember that 'bend' refers to ×1 hip joint only; knees must not bend after push-off.

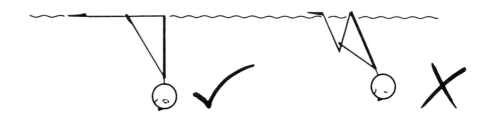

7 Start with head-first surface dive as before. Once on pool-floor, swim along floor four, five or six strokes then re-surface. Where the gymnastic movement of a surface dive is required, ×2 swimming down from the surface is not acceptable.

8 To finish, 4 fast widths (48m) in under 1 minute. Competitive club swimmers in under 49 seconds.
Widths 1 and 3: back crawl.
Widths 2 and 4: breast stroke.

DEEP 8

Equipment

Next week, a complete survival test kit lesson for Bronze and Silver candidates. Golds and Merits should bring practice kit. See kit lists pp. 122 and 123.

Marker brick (not to be picked up or moved) should be placed on pool-floor, next to line, 5 metres from T-mark.
Select a swimmer with good surface diving technique and the ability to swim under water well. This swimmer should demonstrate the HFSD and FFSD and underwater swim as in Bronze and Silver awards. Later in the lesson, the whole group will have a try.

Head-first and feet-first surface dive *(2m maximum depth)*
Swimmer should surface-dive down to touch the T-mark, or other

marker first, swim along pool-floor until hands **pass** *marker brick, then re-surface.*

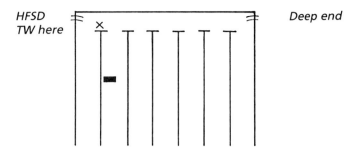

Eyes should be kept open when swimming on pool-floor.

Before a feet-first surface dive, a swimmer would tread water directly above the T-mark.

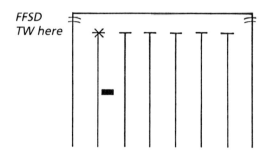

Survival practice kit on. One float on pool-edge.

1 Straight jump off pool-edge, with legs together. Sink into crouch. Tuck head in front of knees and swim along pool-floor three or four strokes. Re-surface and tread water. Return to trough.

2 Swim two fast widths breast stroke.

3 *Timid or unskilled undressers chin-deep. Remainder to 2m depth.* All tread water for one minute, 'shielding eyes from sun' with one hand. Then remove top – and belt – and trousers last. Throw top and belt out. Make a float from trousers and lie back, holding float above thighs for 1 minute.

Throw float out.

4 *2m maximum depth.*
Feet-first surface dive. *By numbers* – 3m from side, tread water, facing across width. Lift arms above head, slide legs together. Sink to pool-floor, keeping back **vertical**, into crouch. Tuck head in front of knees and swim along pool-floor for two or three strokes. Re-surface and swim to far side.

5 *Divide group into four sections.*
Each section to have a marker brick 5 metres from a T-mark.
Everyone hold the deep-end trough.
Explain that everyone is going to practise HFSD and FFSD, and 5m underwater swim, as it would be measured in a survival award. Also, remind swimmers not to hold the trough whilst waiting for their turn during the actual award, but to tread water instead.
Do two surface dives each (one head-first, one feet-first), each dive followed by a swim to the brick on pool-floor, if possible. After re-surfacing, swim back to group. Do not grab hold of trough on re-surfacing.

DEEP 9

Equipment

Next week no extra kit will be needed.
Bronze and silver swimmers – complete survival test kit on. Golds and Merits – practice kit on.
NB Other circuits and markers may have to be devised to suit individual pools.

1 *A practice for survival tests, in a **shortened** form.*

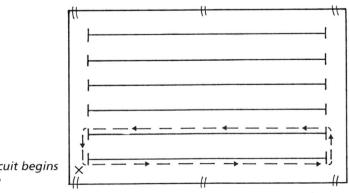

✗ *Circuit begins here*

Use a circuit round two lines, as shown.
Try to complete the following without a rest.

(a) One at a time, straddle entry into pool and swim one circuit, any stroke.

(b) All tread water for 2 minutes. During first minute: **Silvers** shield eyes with one hand, **Golds** wave both arms above head, **Merits** remove gym shoes, then keep afloat holding one foot with opposite hand.

(c) *Anyone still nervous about removing kit in deep water should swim to chin-deep area.*
All remove kit.
Bronzes throw kit out and swim two circuits.
Silvers, Golds and **Merits** make a float with trousers, after throwing rest of kit out.
Silvers float for 1 minute . . . then throw floats out.
Golds and Merits float for 2 minutes . . . then throw floats out.

(d) Everyone to deep-end trough and hold on.
Normally there would be no rest at this point in the test (NB: explain this to children).
Bronzes and Silvers now do two circuits, surface-diving down to T-mark and swimming on pool-floor to brick at the beginning of the second circuit. (See p. 85.) Bronzes do a head-first dive. Silvers do a feet-first dive.
Gold and Merits swim four circuits at a good speed, doing surface dives at the end of each circuit, opposite 5m marker on pool-edge and then swimming along floor to T-mark.
2 surface dives head-first.
2 surface dives feet-first.
All should be swimming round the circuit anti-clockwise but Bronzes and Silvers are surface diving at beginning of circuit; Golds and Merits, at end.

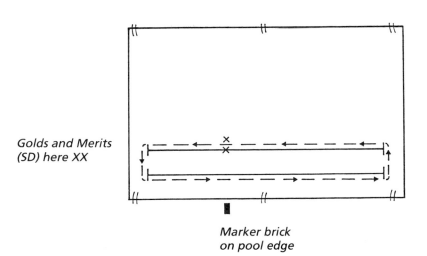

Golds and Merits (SD) here XX

Marker brick on pool edge

(e) All climb out at deep-end, without using trough, after circuits with surface dives are finished.

With any time left, practise the following, choosing your weakest first:

straddle entry

climbing out

float-making

surface diving and 5m swim on floor.

Try to note which swimmers choose to remove kit in chin-deep water. They are not ready for testing.

Arrange tests in Bronze and Silver survival for the next two weeks.

Read test descriptions obtainable from STA (see p. 127).

DEEP GROUP · SECOND TERM

DEEP 10

Equipment

Complete test kit next week (see pp. 122–3).
One float on pool-side; kit should be left off this week.

1 Jump in, taking off from both feet at the same time, entering pool with legs together.

2 With thumbs linked and arms ahead, elbows straight, swim 2 widths non-stop breast stroke, leg action only.
Heels should be lifted to surface when frogging.

3 Keeping legs together and still, swim 2 widths non-stop breast stroke, arm action only.
*Keep hands **ahead** of shoulders throughout. Tuck elbows and upper arms **strongly** into ribs when frogging.*

4 Swim 4 widths non-stop breast stroke, complete stroke. Finish **every** stroke with a glide (I-shape) and tuck head between arms during glide, for blowing out, eyebrows level with surface. Look **ahead**, not down at pool-floor.

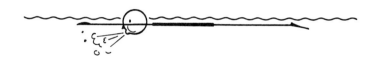

5 On back, back-crawl kick. Count kicks in threes.
On first 1, 2, 3, lift **both** arms at same time up and over to the surface beyond head with elbows straight.
On next 1, 2, 3 sweep **both** arms horizontally round to thighs.
Try to keep backs of hands together during the lift over and the entry into water.

1 width

6 Swim 3 widths non-stop back-crawl. Avoid collisions when turning. Count kicks in threes. Use arms alternately.
For **every** 1, 2, 3, an arm should be entering the water beyond your shoulder and sweeping.

7 *Front crawl practice 5 (see p. 66), breathing on preferred side.*

8 *Front crawl practice 6 (see p. 67), breathing on preferred side.*

9 *Front crawl practice 7 (see p. 67).*

10 In groups of three, transfer to shallow water (less than 1m unless you are very tall) with one float per group. Two should stand facing each other 2m apart. Between them, a float should be held on the surface by the third swimmer. Take it in turns to dive over the float and pass through partner's legs.

Feet together, bend knees, lean over float

Fall forwards and push seat up

Keep arms ahead and head between arms throughout. This is a ×3 each basic standing dive action.

11 *With the remaining time,* return to deep water and practise the following:

(a) tread water for 2 minutes, hands on top of head

(b) a neat head-first surface dive

(c) an underwater swim of five or six strokes.

DEEP 11

Equipment

Next week trousers, belts/elastic. Merits bring a long-sleeved top, too. Marker bricks in position as shown in 6 (p. 92).

Kit on seating, one float on pool-side.
Stand on pool-edge, float behind feet. *Number group in threes or fours.*

1   Straddle entry. Return to trough then swim 2 fast widths life-saving back stroke with hands on opposite shoulders.

2 *Front crawl practice 6 (see p. 67), breathing on preferred side.*

3 *Front crawl practice 7 (see p. 67).*

4 Put kit **on** whilst in deep water, if competent; otherwise work in chin-deep area. (Pile kit on a float in the deep end so it is not necessary to keep swimming to side.)

5 Once fully kitted out, do the following non-stop: 2 widths, breast stroke legs only, holding the float ahead. Put float on pool-side.

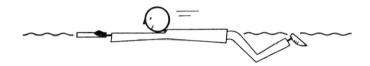

Then, still in deep water, remove shoes (if worn), socks, belts and trousers. Throw out shoes, socks and belts. Make a float with trousers. Once float is inflated, climb out. Remove top.

6

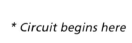

* Circuit begins here

*ˣ Bronzes and
   Silvers
   SD here*

*ˣˣ Golds and Merits
    SD here*

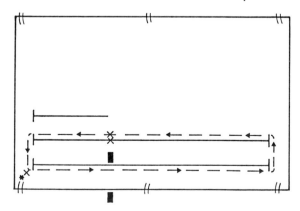

Swim round a two-line circuit as follows: front crawl and/or breast stroke for 5 minutes.
Gold and Merit candidates surface dive towards end of each circuit, opposite marker on pool-edge, and swim 5 metres under water. Surface dives should alternate head first and feet first. In 5 minutes these swimmers should have swum over 160m.

Silvers and Bronzes surface dive at beginning of first and second circuits only, down to T-mark and swim along pool-floor to a 5m marker brick (one head-first dive, one feet-first).

7 Practise sitting or semi-crouching dives at the deep end.
When diving from a semi-crouching stance, entry should be further away from pool-side. The action is the same: 'over a (longer) bridge and down a slide'.

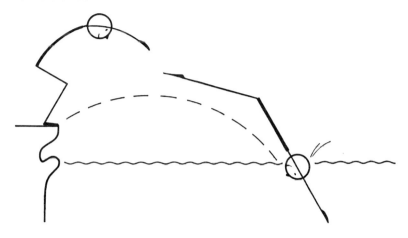

Remember to push **seat** up, to avoid 'touching the bridge'.

DEEP 12

Equipment
Complete test kit next week.
Trousers, belts/elastic on; Merits only to wear long-sleeved top as well. Number group in 3s/4s.

1 Setting off by numbers at 5-second intervals, attempt the following in 2 minutes and 35 seconds:

(a) straddle entry,

(b) 4 widths breast stroke (48m),

(c) remove and throw out elastic

(d) remove trousers and make float.

Call out when each group's finishing time is reached.

2 *A long swim (Merits wear sweaters):*
Bronzes swim 10 widths breast stroke.

Silvers swim 9 widths life-saving back stroke and 1 width breast stroke.
Golds and Merits swim 12 widths any stroke with a time limit of 4 minutes and 30 seconds.
Spread Golds and Merits out, so they may set off at same time.
Golds and Merits do feet-first surface dives only, on widths 4, 8 and 12.
Bronzes and Silvers surface dive on width 2, Bronzes head first, Silvers feet first.
All swimmers do their surface dive(s) at centre of width, then swim 5 metres along pool-floor to touch last line before re-surfacing.
Don't hit the wall!
Merits remove and throw out long-sleeved top.

3 On back, crawl kick at your own preferred speed, arms **straight** and **touching ears**, holding float ahead on surface. Count kicks 1, 2, 3, 1, 2, 3, 1, 2, 3, throughout 2 widths, non-stop. Kick strongly.

4 At deep end pool-edge, sitting or semi-crouching (either way), your body should be leaning over top of imaginary bridge, ready for diving before take-off. Put head between arms.

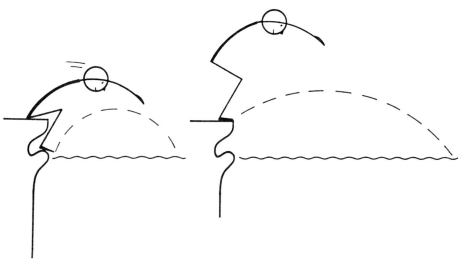

Slide over far side of bridge, pushing seat up a little to lift it over the top of the bridge. Enter water forwards and down, not vertically.

5 *Front crawl practice 1 (see p. 65).*

×2 **6** Front crawl complete stroke. Breathe on preferred side. Blow widths out looking forwards.

DEEP 13

Equipment

No survival kit next week.
This week all in full kit.
Number group in 3s.

1 Straddle entry, then swim 4 widths non-stop. Use a different stroke for each width – that's four strokes altogether.

2 Any merit survival swimmers should now try a timed swim over 4 lengths.
(100m should take no longer than 2 minutes and 30 seconds.)

3 All others tread water for 3 minutes.

(a) 1 minute waving arms above head.

(b) 1 minute using arms as well as legs.

(c) 1 minute with hands on top of head.

4 Merits remove and throw out gym shoes and socks, then keep afloat for 1 minute rubbing one foot with the opposite hand.
Meanwhile all others remove kit and throw out everything but the trousers; make a float and float with it for:
2 minutes – Gold
1 minute – Silvers
30 seconds – Bronzes.

5 Merits (still in clothes) and Golds swim round circuit for 10 minutes, non-stop, surface-diving towards end of every circuit and swimming 5 metres under the surface (try to complete 320 metres in 10 minutes).

Bronze and Silvers meanwhile do the following:

three surface-dives to a T-mark, each followed by a 5-metre swim along the pool-floor to a marker brick.
Bronzes do 2 head-first and 1 feet-first dives.
Silvers do 1 head-first and 2 feet-first dives.

Underwater swimming *coaching points. Encourage a pull to the thighs and then a stretch forwards until arms are straight and hands together. Keep head down and eyes* **open.** *There are two glides in an underwater stroke, following the pull and following the stretch forwards.*

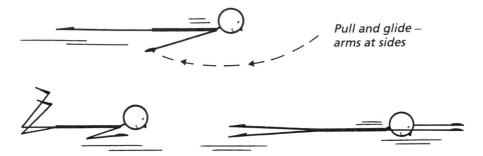

Pull and glide – arms at sides

Forward and glide – arms ahead

6 Bronzes and Silvers continue with *(Golds and Merits should still be doing circuits!):*

(a) 2 **good** straddle entries.

(b) 2 sitting or semi-crouching dives.

7 *All change!*
Bronzes and Silvers swim round circuit **without** surface-diving for 5 minutes, non-stop. Silvers use life-saving back stroke or back-crawl throughout, Bronzes use breast stroke.

Golds and Merits (remove kit first) do two good straddle entries, and two sitting or semi-crouching dives.

DEEP 14

Equipment

No kit on. Number group in twos or threes.
Strokes' practice.

1 Stand on pool-edge. By numbers either dive in or do straddle entry, but try not to submerge more than half a metre below surface. Return to side.

2 *Front crawl practice 1 (p. 65).*
2 widths Concentrate on keeping float **in front** of you, so working arm each arm enters water forwards and at full stretch.

3 *Front crawl practice 4 (p. 66), turning head always to preferred*
2 widths *breathing side.*

2 widths **4** *Front crawl practice 5 (p. 67), breathing on preferred side.*

1 width **5** Front crawl practice 6 (p. 67).

6 Unsupported front crawl: 3 widths non-stop, breathing on preferred side.

7 Swim **fast**, with hands on hips, 4 widths life-saving back stroke. Keep thighs and body along surface throughout. Do not allow hips to sink from surface or knees to bend upwards through surface.

8 In pairs and both holding the same float, one partner tows the other for 2 widths non-stop.
Person towing should use life-saving back stroke. Person being towed lies **still** on tummy. Both hold float in two hands tightly, elbows **straight.**

Propulsion must be strong. Keep up a constant speed over the distance (24m) and work hard.
Change over.

DEEP 15

Equipment

Next week: bring survival practice kit.
One float each. Number group in 2s/3s.

1 Stand on pool-edge (1.8–2m). Try a crouch dive in **forwards** and downwards. Swim near pool-floor for three good pulls, then mushroom-float to surface. Swim breast stroke to far side.

2 Non-stop, swim 5 widths life-saving back stroke.
Widths 1 and 2 – hands on opposite shoulders.
Widths 3 and 4 – with arms extended sideways and in line with shoulders.

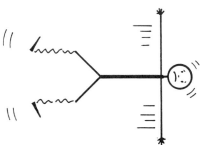

Last width – using arms to scull as well, as fast as possible.

1 width **3** *Front crawl practice 6 (p. 67) breathing to preferred side.*

4 *Remind swimmers to **turn** and not lift head for breathing in, then repeat front crawl practice 6.*

5 2 widths front crawl, without floats. Try to maintain a smooth arm action, in spite of turning head to breathe in.

6 *At 1.8–2m, practise smooth approach to HFSD.*
Hold trough behind with both hands, feet against wall. Push off, hands moving ahead. Do two complete breast strokes, i.e. pull and glide, pull and glide, then straight into pull, bend and lift (surface dive). There should be no pause between the second glide and the surface dive.
Remember that the word 'bend' applies to the hip joint, **not** the knees.
Try to maintain a stretched feeling from finger-tips to toes
×2 during descent to pool-floor, then re-surface.

7 *Deep end pool-edge for diving.*
Stress the safety aspects:

- **forward** and down entry.
- head **down** between arms.
- keep arms extended ahead whilst going towards floor.

Semi-crouching dives for whole group (sitting dives for any who are still nervous). Free practice.

Think:
'Over a bridge and down a slide'.
Remember to push **seat** upwards, not feet, when leaving pool-edge.
Select and inform those who perform good semi-crouching dives, with an 'over-bridge' flight and a safe, neat entry, to do standing dives next week.

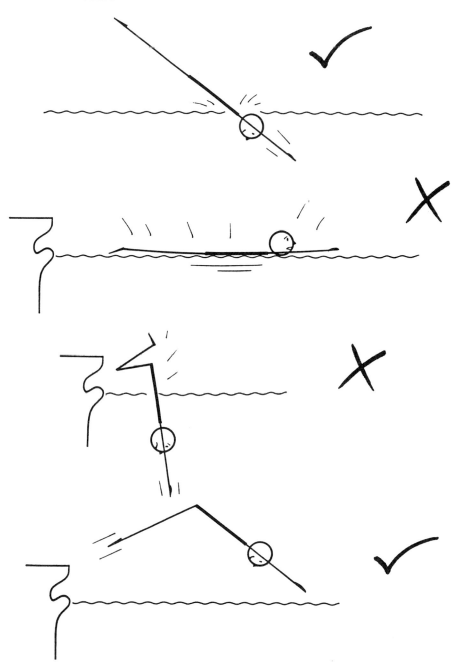

8 Four widths back crawl in 45 seconds; no collisions when turning.

DEEP 16

Equipment

Next week: bring survival practice kit.
Practice kit on, one float each.
Stand on edge of pool at 1.8–2m. Number group in threes.

1 Dive in from a semi-crouching position, forwards and down. Close to pool-floor swim four strokes, then mushroom-float to surface. When your back re-surfaces, count 4 seconds with your head **down** before swimming to far side.

2 Swim to a space in deep water, and tread water. Remove kit and throw out all except trousers. Make a float in no more than 35 seconds. When time is up, throw float out.

3 Return to original places at side.
2 widths *Front crawl practice 6 (see p. 67), breathing to preferred side.*

4 Unsupported front crawl, breathing to preferred side. Make
2 widths sure that hands are pushing back through water to thighs.

5 In threes: one swimmer, using life-saving back stroke, should tow the other two for 2 widths. Change places until everyone has had a turn at towing.

6 Beginning at trough, push off and:
pull and glide – pull and glide
pull bend and lift (HFSD).
Remember that 'bend' refers to hips not knees. Keep legs together.
×2 Once on pool-floor swim one stroke forwards, then re-surface.

7 *Sitting, semi-crouching or standing dives from deep end. (5 mins.)*
Those swimmers selected for standing dives (end of last week's lesson) now stand on edge in Y position, with head **up**.

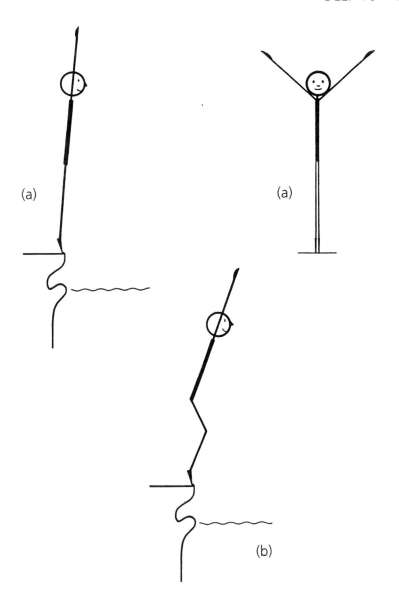

(a)

(a)

(b)

(a) Rise on to toes and balance, briefly.

(b) Topple forwards to gain some momentum. Bend the knees and . . .

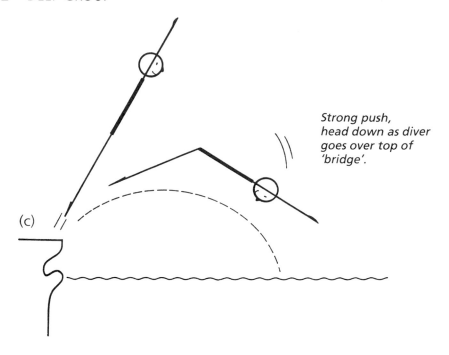

*Strong push,
head down as diver
goes over top of
'bridge'.*

(c)

(c) . . . **push** up over bridge. Head should go down **after** take-off. Bring your hands together for entry.

8 (a) Do a head-first surface dive after three complete breast strokes, i.e.:
pull and glide
pull and glide
pull and glide
pull, bend and lift.

9 Swim 4 widths back crawl non-stop (no collisions, please).
Feet must leave a foamy trail on surface.
Arms and hands must make no splash at all.

DEEP 17

Equipment

*Next week: bring survival practice kit.
Practice kit on. One float each.*

1 Dive in, down and forwards towards pool-floor. Swim one stroke forwards along floor, mushroom-float to surface, swim one stroke forwards on surface (pull and glide), then head-first surface dive to floor and swim along floor to last line – re-surface carefully.

2 Swim 4 widths non-stop using life-saving back stroke with hands on opposite shoulders. No collisions!

3 At deep end, tread water for 2 minutes rubbing one foot with opposite hand.

4 Remove kit and throw out apart from trousers. Make a float in no more than 35 seconds. Then link arms with another swimmer and together kick 2 widths. Hold on to your own float with both hands.

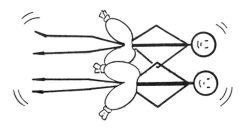

5 Swim 4 widths front crawl non-stop, breathing in on preferred side. Think 'breathe' when breathing in and 'blow' when blowing out.
Slide hand into water ahead of same shoulder, i.e. right hand in front of right shoulder.

6 Hold trough behind with both hands; feet against wall. Push off and swim three complete breast-strokes, i.e. pull and glide three times.
Then head-first surface dive – pull, bend and lift.
Swim along floor to next line, picking up an imaginary brick with both hands. Re-surface, holding 'brick' close to body.
×2 Turn on to back and complete the width (holding 'brick' under chin with both hands) using life-saving back stroke.

7 *Diving practice, as in previous lesson (see pp. 101–2), for 5 minutes.*

DEEP GROUP · THIRD TERM

DEEP 18

Equipment

Next week: bring complete survival kit.
Practice kit on.
Number group in 3s/4s.

Stand on pool-edge at side of deep end.

Non-stop:
1 Dive in. Swim 1 width (12m) breast stroke. Climb out.
Dive in. Swim 1 width near pool-floor. Climb out.
Dive in. Swim 1 width breast stroke. Climb out.
Dive in. Swim 1 width front crawl. Hold trough.

2 In a space in the deep water, remove trousers (Merits: gym shoes and trousers). Make a float in less than 30 seconds. Then, on tummy with float under chin, crawl kick 4 widths non-stop.

3 Throw out float and the rest of your kit whilst treading water. Return to original places at side.

4 *Feet-first surface dive practice.* **Tread water about 3 metres from side, facing across pool. With an extra strong push from legs and arms, force body up above surface, then raise arms above head, slide feet together and sink into crouch on pool-floor. Do not lean forwards or backwards whilst sinking; keep back vertical.**
×3 Return to side.

5 *Smooth approach to FFSD.* **Push off and swim two complete breast strokes forwards. Then, pulling both arms downwards and lifting head, swing bent knees forwards under body. Once body is upright do feet-first surface dive** – pull and glide, pull
×2 and glide, swing forwards, arms up and sink.

Glide

Swing forwards

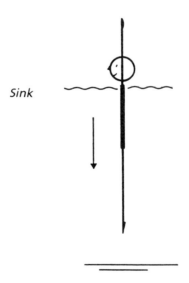

Sink

6 Practising neat dive from deep-end edge (5 mins).
Remind swimmers always to enter pool **forwards** and
downwards. Vertical entries from the side are only for official
diving areas with at least 3 metres of water.
Try to keep feet and legs tightly pressed together throughout
take-off, flight and entry.
Kicking feet up behind one at a time can cause a painful
overswing of legs on entry. Push your seat into the air instead.
Your legs will follow the flight path and entry will be
comfortable.

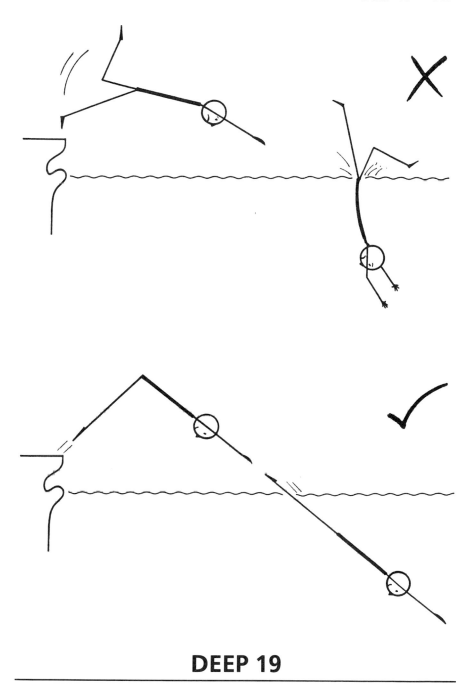

DEEP 19

Surface diving

Explain briefly that survival awards are swum in circuits, so swimmers do not touch pool-side during test. When doing surface dives **Bronzes and Silvers** *surface dive down towards a T-mark, and swim along pool-floor until their hands pass a brick 5m from T-mark, at* **beginning** *of circuit.*

Golds and Merits surface dive opposite a brick on the pool-side and re-surface with hands above T-mark, at **end** of each circuit. During surface diving and underwater swims, care must be taken not to touch the pool-floor. When re-surfacing, do not push off from floor.

* Circuit begins

ˣ Bronzes and Silvers surface dive here

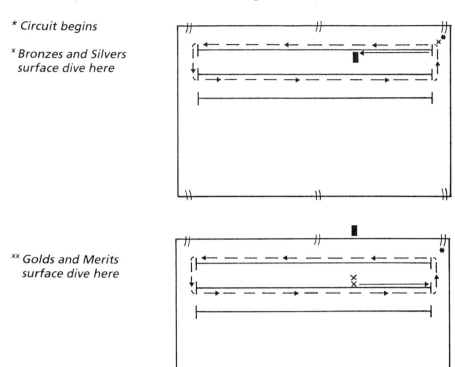

ˣˣ Golds and Merits surface dive here

Equipment

Next week: bring survival practice kit.
Complete test kit on. Marker-bricks in position as illustrated.

1 Merits and Golds – swim 4 lengths (100m) timed. Swim fast.
Merits try for 2 minutes and 30 seconds.
Golds try for 4 minutes.

Meanwhile, **Silvers and Bronzes:**
(a) straddle entry, landing well away from pool-side.
(b) tread water for 2 minutes.
Silvers shield eyes from sun with one hand.
Bronzes – hands on hips.

2 Merits remove and throw out gym shoes and socks. Then swim 11 circuits round two lines (500m) non-stop, surface diving on the first 6 circuits and swimming 5 metres under water, as described at beginning of lesson.
(3 surface dives head first, 3 feet first.)

Meanwhile, **Golds and Silvers** remove and throw out kit, keeping trousers. Make a float and lie back under it for 3 minutes.

×6 **Bronzes** remove kit and throw out, then practise straddle entry.

Climb out over side without using trough before each straddle entry.

3 Merits should still be doing circuits.
Golds now join the Merits and attempt to do 5 circuits (approx. 225m) in 7 minutes, surface diving feet first at the end of each circuit, and swimming 5 metres under surface after each dive.
Away from circuit areas, **Silvers and Bronzes** practise surface diving down to a T-mark then swimming along floor to a marker brick 5 metres from the T-mark.
Bronzes 4 head-first surface dives.
Silvers 2 head-first surface dives and 2 feet-first surface dives.

4 In the time which remains, do as much as possible of the following:

(a) tow a partner 1 half-length using a float and life-saving back stroke.

(b) 2 neat standing or semi-crouching dives from deep end pool-side.

(c) make sure no one in water is in your way, then stand on pool-edge, holding your trousers, close your eyes and jump in. Keep your eyes closed until you have made a float.

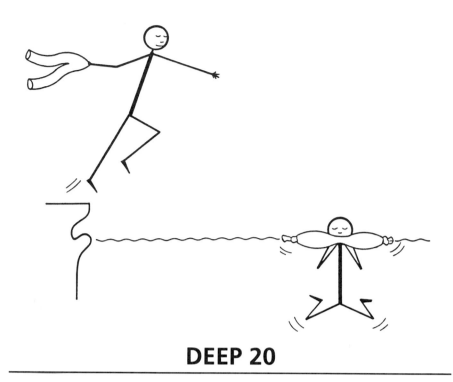

DEEP 20

Equipment

After this lesson, complete survival kit will be required only by swimmers taking part in testing. Survival practice kit on. Bricks and floats to hand.
Number group in 2s/3s.
Stand on pool-edge.
1 Straddle entry into pool, and swim non-stop 6 widths breast-stroke. At the centre of width 3, surface dive feet first to pool-floor and swim 5 metres along floor to the side. Re-surface.
Swim the whole of width 6 (12m) under water, pushing off from pool-wall to begin with.

2 Tread water. Remove kit and throw out, apart from trousers. Try to make a float in 25 seconds. Lie back and float with it for 3 minutes. Throw it out.

3 Tow a partner using a float and life-saving back stroke for four widths. You are also carrying the suitcase!

4 Swim **non-stop** 2 lengths front crawl, thinking: breathe, blow, breathe, blow – one word for each time an elbow lifts out of water. Remember, turning your head to breathe must not affect the smoothness of your stroke.

5 In twos or threes, each pair or group with a brick **tread water** close together, one swimmer holding brick in both hands.
After treading water for 20 seconds, this swimmer should pass the brick through legs to partner, who then repeats the process. Keep repeating the whole exercise for 2 minutes.

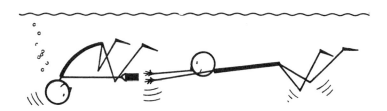

6 Swim non-stop back crawl for 3 minutes (in widths). Leave foamy trail on surface from toes. Use both arms simultaneously for pulling. No collisions!

7 Swim 2 lengths (50m) back crawl non-stop, using arms alternately. Take arms over close to ears.

8 Face wall and hold trough with both hands. Let go and sink vertically into a crouch. Roll back, placing one foot against wall.

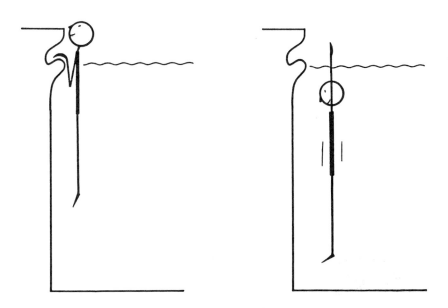

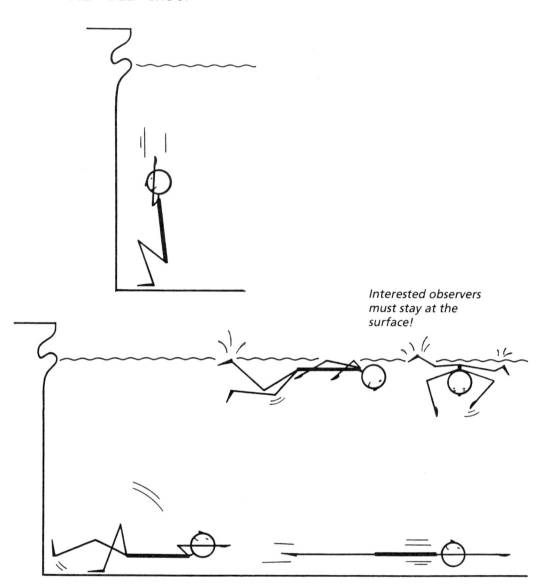

Interested observers must stay at the surface!

Push off and with head back and arms stretched try to glide along pool-floor for about 3 metres.

9 Do 3 very neat standing dives to finish. Leave pool-edge with a controlled push up of seat, both legs together. Entry is **forwards**, never straight down. Enter water with head down between arms. Keep arms ahead whilst going towards pool-floor.
The last three lesson plans can be displayed on a wall, for the deep group swimmers to read and work through on their own.
This will enable one of the teachers to be used in testing awards.

Any deep group working independently must be competent in deep water and must be capable of working sensibly and quietly. Inform the life guard of this situation.

DEEP 21

Equipment

Next week: bring pyjama trousers only.
No survival kit on. One float each. Bricks to hand.

1 A vertical jump, sinking to crouch. At pool-floor level do one **slow** forward somersault, re-surface, then swim breast stroke to far side. On the way, do a head-first surface dive very neatly; no underwater swim.

2 Non-stop swimming for 5 minutes, using back crawl and life-saving back stroke (hands on hips) – two widths (24m) each stroke. Repeat strokes in same order until 5 minutes have elapsed. Try to maintain a steady pace. No collisions!

3 Holding a float ahead of you, swim supported front crawl, thinking 'breathe, blow, breathe, blow' (one word per arm-lift). Use head correctly, i.e. turn it to preferred side on 'breathe', look ahead on 'blow'.

4 widths

4 Still using float, try bi-lateral breathing as follows. Think 'breathe, blow, blow, breathe, blow, blow' (one word per arm-lift). Use your head correctly. Your head should now look forwards during two arm lifts, giving you longer to blow out. You will breathe in on a different side each time.

widths

5 Front crawl, without a float, 2 widths non-stop. Decide on either 'breathe, blow, breathe, blow' or 'breathe, blow, blow, breathe, blow, blow'.

6 Swim 6 widths breast stroke. Finish every stroke with a glide. (Remember Y, frog I, Y, frog I.) Each width (12m) must be crossed in no more than 10 complete strokes. On every glide (I), as shoulders submerge, blow into water, looking ahead.

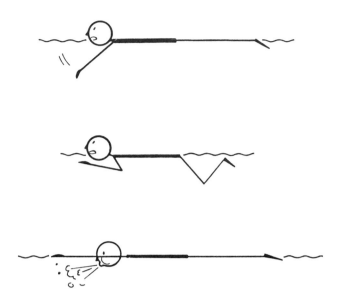

No exaggerated ducking and lifting of the head.
The head rises with the pull and lowers with the glide, but
should not nod.

7 Drop brick carefully in 1.8m depth, centre of width.
Swim breast stroke from trough towards brick for two or three
pull and glides.
Head-first surface dive to pool-floor, swim forward to brick
along floor, and grasp brick with both hands. Re-surface. Return
to side using life-saving back stroke, carrying brick just below
chin with both hands.
If surface dive is completed **well before** brick, you can
concentrate on producing a neat surface dive, knowing you will
×3 not overshoot brick, before reaching pool-floor.

DEEP 22

No survival practice kit on. *Bricks, weighted hoops, empty plastic
containers and pyjama trousers to hand.*

1 Stand on edge, gripping it with toes. Jump upwards and
forwards as high as possible. Whilst in the air, do a 'pike' action:
swing your legs up level with your hips, keeping knees **straight**
×3 and touch toes with fingers. Then straighten for entry.

2 Swim non-stop using life-saving back stroke 8 half-lengths or 16 half-widths (100m).
For 2 half-lengths (4 half-widths) you must carry a large brick in both hands above your chest.

3 Swim non-stop front crawl 8 half-lengths or 16 half-widths. Use 'breathe, blow, blow' if you know how to. If not, remember to breathe in looking back at one shoulder; to blow out, looking forwards with eyebrows level with surface.

4 Tread water for 4 minutes holding a brick, or a plastic container half full of water, on one shoulder.

You may change shoulders!

5 In pairs, swim either 8 half-lengths or 16 half-widths (100m) using breast stroke. On 4 and 5 (or 3, 4, 5 and 6 if doing 16 half-widths), take it in turns to float on your back, with your hands on your partner's shoulders, and be pushed along.

Swimmer lying back, hands on partner's shoulders, elbows straight

6 Fold trousers neatly into the smallest possible bundle. Hold the bundle in your teeth and straddle entry into pool without wetting the bundle! Then, whilst treading water, make a float in less than 30 seconds.
Kick 4 half-lengths on tummy, with float under chin.

7 With a partner counting seconds aloud, attempt to mushroom-float for 17 seconds without lifting head. Change over.

8 Surface dive head first down to a T-mark, then swim along pool-floor and through a hoop 6 metres from T-mark before re-surfacing.

9 Flat on your back, on the surface, without moving, float for 1 minute. At the end of the minute, quickly 'pike' and attempt to sink at least 1 metre.

This is a pike position

10 Swim, non-stop, 4 half-lengths (50m) back crawl. On the first 2, pull with both arms simultaneously; on the last 2, pull with alternate arms. No collisions!

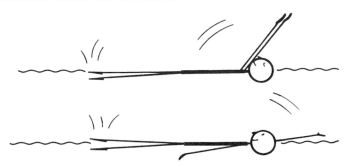

11 Dive from pool-edge:

(a) over 1 bridge (imaginary)

(b) over 2

(c) over 3.

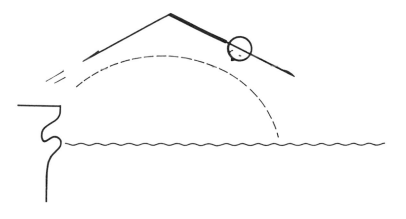

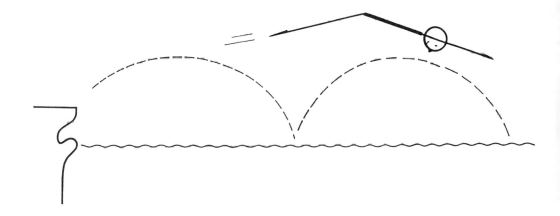

DEEP 23

Equipment

Weighted hoops and bricks to hand.

1 Stand on pool-edge at deep end.
Dive in and, in 2 minutes and 30 seconds, swim breast stroke:

(a) 1 length or 2 half-lengths (25m), arms only

(b) 1 length breast stroke, legs only, and

(c) 2 lengths (50m) complete stroke.

2 Stand on pool-edge.
Do a neat vertical jump with legs together, sinking to crouch on pool-floor.
Mushroom-float to surface.
Stretch into a glide position – head down.
Roll on to back and float for 30 seconds without moving.

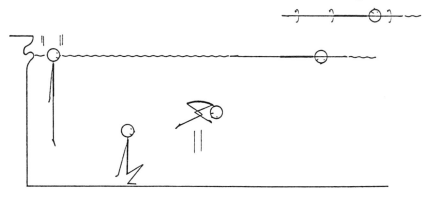

3 Beginning with a shallow dive, can you swim 25m front-crawl in 23 seconds?
(If you are a competition swimmer, i.e. a member of a club, can you do the swim in 18 seconds?)

4 In 1.8m depth, place a weighted hoop on pool-floor as illustrated. Tread water 4m from hoop, holding a brick close to chest.
Feet-first surface dive to floor, then swim, carrying brick, along floor and through hoop and re-surface.

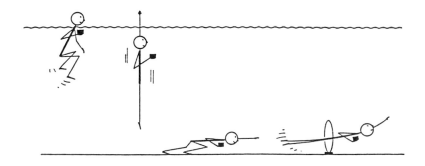

5 In deep end, if water level is not too low (30cm maximum below pool-edge) enter:

(a) knees first

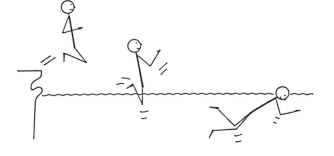

(b) seat first
(push **away** from edge)

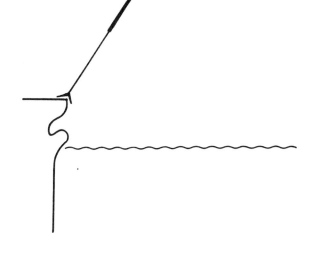

(c) sideways
(hold ears on).

6 Scull (hands only) for 10m:

(a) on your back, head first

(b) on your back, feet first

(c) on your tummy, feet first.

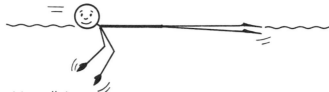

Don't forget to smile!

7 Swim 25m back crawl in 25 seconds
(club swimmers – 20 seconds).

8 With a partner counting seconds aloud, mushroom-float for 15 seconds; lift head, breathe in, head down and MF for a further 7 seconds. Change over.

9 In 1.8m, tread water with your back to a weighted hoop (on floor). Feet-first surface dive into crouch. Somersault **slowly** backwards and scull backwards feet-first through hoop; then re-surface.

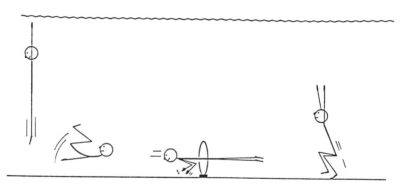

10 Surface-dive head first, keeping legs together and lifting legs from surface with knees straight. Before legs sink beneath surface, swing them apart and together again.

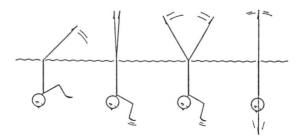

11 Dive in and swim 6 lengths (150m) in 4 minutes and 30 seconds.

APPENDIX

EDUCATION COMMITTEE GUIDANCE ON CONDITIONS GOVERNING THE AWARD OF SWIMMING BADGES

The following are based on Cumbria Education Committee swimming awards. Pool instructors should also receive a copy with accompanying notes on the testing requirements.

BEGINNERS (Yellow)

Swim 1 width or 10m using any stroke.

IMPROVERS (Blue)

1 Swim 25m front crawl **or** back crawl **or** breast stroke **or** life-saving back stroke.
2 Recover an object from bottom of pool in 1m depth of water.
3 Tread water for 30 seconds.

INTERMEDIATE (Green)

1 Continuously swim 25m front crawl or breast stroke **and** 25m back crawl or life-saving back stroke.
2 Vertical jump from pool-edge, sink and crouch on floor, re-surface and tread water for 1 minute, then swim to side.
3 Swim 2 widths continuously; first width on front, second width on back. At centre of pool on each width, change to a face-down, stationary floating position for 5 seconds before completing width.
4 From side, push down head-first, and swim to touch point on pool bottom with both hands, re-surface and swim to side. (Point – 4m from side.)

PROFICIENCY (Red)

Note 1, 2, and 3 should be completed without stopping to rest.

1 Straddle entry into deep end.
2 Swim 50m breast stroke **and**
        50m one back stroke **and**
        50m free style.
3 Tread water 1.8m for 1 minute then, raising arms above head and sliding legs together, sink feet-first into crouch on pool-floor. Re-surface and tread water for a further minute.
4 Head-first surface dive to touch pool bottom with both hands. Return to surface.

ADVANCED (White)

Note 1, 2, 3, 4, and 5 should be completed without a rest.

Clothing — Pyjama, or lightweight trousers, T-shirt and socks.

1 In clothing, enter water with a shallow dive.
2 Swim 50m any stroke.
3 Remove clothing and throw it out, without support.
4 Tread water for 2 minutes, hands on opposite shoulders for first minute.
5 Swim continuously 50m front crawl
50m breast stroke
50m any back stroke.
6 Head-first surface dive to pick up a brick with **both** hands from pool-floor and carry it, using life-saving back stroke, to the side.

BRONZE AND SILVER COMPLETE SURVIVAL TEST KIT

Bronzes and Silvers wear:

1 long-sleeved button-front tops
2 pyjama trousers; full-length leg
3 elasticated belt, or strip tied to fit waist.

Silvers wear in addition:

4 a T-shirt or vest.

Note: survival practice kit items are labelled with a 'P'.

GOLD AND MERIT COMPLETE SURVIVAL TEST KIT

Golds and Merits wear almost the same kit.

Merits must wear proper trousers or a skirt — not pyjama trousers — and gym shoes.

Golds — 7 items.

Merits — 8 items.

Note: survival practice kit items are labelled with a 'P'.

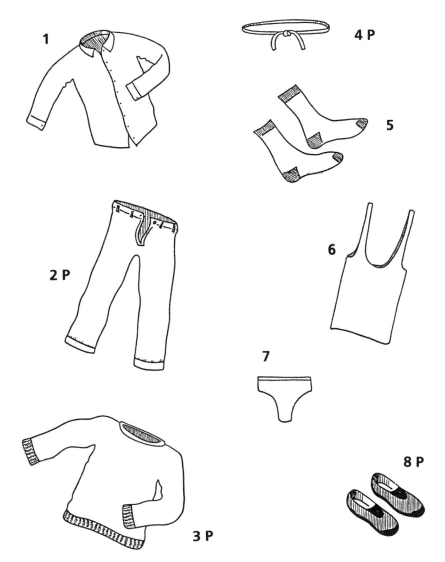

Swimming awards gained 19 /19
School ....

STA Survival Awards
(Fill in every award gained this school year Sept.   to June   .)

Year	N.O.R.	M	G	S	B	A	P	Int	Imp	Be	NS
6											
5											
4											
Total											

or (between 6 and 5), or (between 5 and 4)

STA (or ASA) Distance awards.
(Fill in every child's maximum distance swum this school year Sept. to June   .)

Year	N.O.R.	1500	1000	800	600	400	200	100	50	25	10	5
6												
5												
4												
Total												

or (between 6 and 5), or (between 5 and 4)

STA (or ASA) Long distance.
(Maximum distance this year)

Year	5km	3km	Other
6			
5			
4			
Total			

or (between 6 and 5), or (between 5 and 4)

Year	C.C.S.
6	
5	
4	
Total	

KEY
N.O.R. Number on roll
N.S. Non-swimmer
C.C.S. Competitive Club
        swimmer attending
        training each week
M Merit **A** Advanced
G Gold **P** Proficiency
S Silver **Int** Intermediate
B Bronze **Imp** Improvers
Be Beginners

ORGANISATION OF SWIMMING INSTRUCTION FOR SCHOOLS

The following instructions and suggestions are intended to eliminate a number of discrepancies and misunderstandings which may occur, and generally to facilitate the teaching of swimming for schools.
Information will be found under the following headings:
- General rules
- Pool safety
- Responsibilities.

General rules

In order to maintain a high standard of cleanliness and to safeguard the health of pupils, you are asked to observe the following rules.

a Each child should bring a towel, swimming costume, comb, handkerchief, warm clothes and waterproof container to carry wet apparel. Pupils with long hair should bring a bathing cap.

b Each child should ensure that body, hair, nails and so on are clean. Hair cream and make-up should not be worn.

c Each child should use the toilet and showers before leaving the changing rooms prior to going on to the pool-side.

d Handkerchiefs should be used before leaving the changing rooms to go on to the pool-side.

e No child should be allowed to enter the pool with a severe cold, cuts, septic spots, ear complaints, a bandaged wound, of if advised by a doctor not to do so.

f Costumes or trunks should not be worn to come to the pool, and children should change on arrival. Clothing other than proper swimming costumes or trunks will not be permitted unless specifically requested (i.e. for personal survival training).

g Children must **ALWAYS** go through the footwash on leaving the changing rooms before going on to the pool-side and on returning to the changing rooms.

h Outdoor shoes *must not* be worn on pool-side by anyone.

i No food or drink must be brought into the premises.

j Jewellery *must not* be worn in the water or on the pool-side, e.g. watches, rings, necklaces.

k Children should be well dried before leaving the changing rooms after a swimming lesson. A small piece of towel to stand on before drying the feet is helpful. Special attention should be given to drying hair, ears and between toes.

l Costumes should be washed, not merely rinsed, at home.

m Children should use the lockers, where provided, for the safe-keeping of their clothes. Money will be required by each child to enable them to use the lockers — this will be refunded when the locker is opened. Clothes are not to be left in cubicles or loose on pegs.

n The owners of the pool accept no responsibility for the safe-keeping of chidren's clothes and personal possessions – remember there could well be members of the public using the changing rooms at the same time.
o The wearing of goggles should only be allowed in exceptional circumstances and only if accompanied by a medical certificate or parent's note.

Pool safety

At all school-use time it is essential that a member of pool staff attends for life-guard duties.
To avoid danger to pupils and other pool users and to avoid wasting time, the following should be noted.
a Children must not be allowed to run along the pool-side.
b No unnecessary talking or noise will be tolerated.
c Pushing, pulling, splashing of one child by another will not be allowed.
d No child will be allowed into the pool-hall without the swimming teacher's presence, or into the water without the swimming teacher's permission.
e Children should always be aware of the swimming teacher's requirements and demands. A system of whistles may facilitate this.
f No child wearing any buoyancy equipment will be allowed in the deep end of the pool. (Life-jacket excepted.)

Responsibilities

a Teachers accompanying children to the pool should aways be present at the pool-side during the lesson given by an instructor and not occupied elsewhere, other than in matters relating to pupils changing. Their function is not only to be responsible for the supervision of the children throughout the time spent at the pool, but also to ensure a second adult is present. Teachers should inform swimming instructors of any children suffering from the following illnesses – asthma, diabetes, epilepsy, heart conditions, dermatitis. Please note – a second adult is of little use in an emergency if he or she is not adequately prepared. Remember a child can drown in less time than it takes to remove a jacket. The pool is large and water supervision is of paramount importance. There can be no hesitation in entering the water to assist a child in difficulties, *so appropriate clothing would be advisable*, e.g. tracksuit, shorts and T-shirt or swimming costume.

Entering the water in emergencies
This should be clearly recognised as a last resort.
The 'Reach, Throw, Wade' instruction is still relevant in swimming pools. Only after these have been tried should the rescuer enter the water. An ill-equipped, poorly trained, less-than-confident rescuer can become another victim.
b The lesson and its contents are the responsibility of the swimming teacher who must be assisted by the accompanying teacher.
c Both class teacher and swimming teacher must be continuously on the alert to prevent behaviour liable to be dangerous or detrimental in any way to those attending lessons.

d It is the responsibility of an accompanying teacher to supervise those children not actually involved in the lessons.

e In the event of an accident or injury, the pool staff are to be advised immediately.

f Attendance registers must be kept by the swimming teacher or the accompanying teacher in case of fire, accident, irregular attendance, and for recording attainment levels.

USEFUL ADDRESSES

1 Swimming Teachers' Association (Awards' Department)
Anchor House
Birch Street
Walsall
WS2 8HZ

2 Amateur Swimming Association
Harold Fern House
Derby Square
Loughborough
Leicestershire
LE11 0AL

3 Royal Life Saving Society
Mountbatten House
Studley
Warwickshire
B80 7NN

Reminder

The 'bible' for swimming pool safety is *Safety in Swimming Pools* by the Health and Safety Commission and approved by the Sports Council.

INDEX